嵩山少林寺武术馆武术教材

焦红波 主编

第二册

【内容简介】 本书主要包括少林大洪拳、少林罗汉拳、少林长拳、少林七星拳、少林单刀和少林十三枪等内容,对少林武术的传播发展,起到很大的促进作用。

适用于业界人士和少林武术研修者,可成为广大少林武术爱好者的良师善友、得力助手。

图书在版编目(CIP)数据

嵩山少林寺武术馆武术教材. 第二册 / 焦红波主编. — 西安:西北工业大学出版社,2016.12
 ISBN 978-7-5612-5168-3

Ⅰ. ①嵩… Ⅱ. ①焦… Ⅲ. ①少林武术-教材 Ⅳ. ①G852

中国版本图书馆 CIP 数据核字(2016)第 290416 号

出版发行:西北工业大学出版社
通信地址:西安市友谊西路 127 号　邮编:710072
电　　话:(029)88493844　88491757
网　　址:www.nwpup.com
印　刷　者:陕西金德佳印务有限公司
开　　本:787 mm×1 092 mm　　1/16
印　　张:17.5
字　　数:311 千字
版　　次:2016 年 12 月第 1 版　2016 年 12 月第 1 次印刷
定　　价:48.00 元

编委会成员
Editorial Board Members

主 编：焦红波
Chief Editor：Jiao Hongbo

副主编：陈俊杰　　王松伟　　王占洋　　郑跃峰
Associate Editor：Chen Junjie　Wang Songwei　Wang Zhanyang　Zheng Yuefeng

执 笔：陈俊杰
Written by：Chen Junjie

编 委：
Editorial Board Members：

阎治军　　韩新强　　王占通　　焦晓伟
Yan Zhijun　Han Xinqiang　Wang Zhantong　Jiao Xiaowei
焦宏敏　　蒋东旭　　吕宏军　　李振亮
Jiao Hongmin　Jiang Dongxu　Lü Hongjun　Li Zhenliang
景冠飞　　刘珊珊　　吴卫永　　董 伟
Jing Guanfei　Liu Shanshan　Wu Weiyong　Dong Wei

翻 译：李广升　　陈中纪
Translator：Li Guangsheng　Chen Zhongji

正宗拳譜
武藝之源

茅高枼

嵩山少林寺武術館

傳承武術文化
振奮民族精神

徐才
乙酉季秋

重振少林雄风
为中华武术奉献
新作贡献

张燮林 题

承先启后 弘扬武学

一九九四年二月廿六日
嵩山少林寺武术馆惠存

香港梁敬武龙有志题
林焕桓题

序

寇武江[①]

  缘于工作我与同事一起到嵩山少林寺武术馆调研,在观看队员表演练功后,红波告诉我,武术馆拟出版一本少林武术教材,并希望我能为之作序。说实话,近段时间对于武术文化与旅游的研究,我虽然下了一点功夫,但对少林武术的套路招式技法学习我可是一窍不通。然而,考虑到出版教材,传承文化,规范练习,是件功在当今、利在后人的好事,我便答应了。

  少林武术在河南旅游文化品牌中极具代表性,在国内外享有盛名。自北魏以来,少林武术伴随着少林寺禅宗的发展,历经1 500多年的沧桑岁月,积淀了丰富而深厚的文化内涵。20世纪80年代,国家旅游局和河南省人民政府共同投资兴建少林寺武术馆时,就依托少林寺"拳以寺名,寺以武显"的文化内涵,将演武厅列入中原旅游区重点工程项目进行建设。其目的是宣传弘扬深厚的河南文化,满足广大武术爱好者和游客学习少林武术和观看少林武术表演的要求。武术馆自1988年开馆至今,以少林武术这一独特的旅游文化为基础,积极开展少林武术国际文化交流和武术教学研究活动,推动了少林武术专项游,吸引了国内外成千上万的武术爱好者前来参观、学习少林武术,培养出了一大批高层次的少林武术专业人才,为宣传弘扬少林武术文化,促进河南旅游业可持续发展做出了突出贡献。

  少林寺在历史上屡遭兵燹,几经兴衰,少林武术也屡遭摧残,濒临失传。20世纪80年代,国家对传统武术文化给予了高度重视,对长期保存于少林高僧及民间武术名师中的珍贵少林武术资料进行了挖掘收集整理,以不同的方式予以出版发行,对少林武术的传播发展起到很大的促进作用,但以教材的形式出版的则很少。

  少林寺武术馆集聚着众多少林武术名家及武坛精英,他们在工作之余

---

① 寇武江:河南省旅游局局长。

长期致力于少林武术文化的研究,并把研究成果在实践中加以验证,不断地修正传统套路中技法理论及技法运用。本书就是他们对少林武术文化研究的成果和近30年来长期从事表演、教学、交流工作经验的积累结晶。我相信本书出版以后,一定会给业界人士和广大少林武术研修者提供一个好的参考,成为广大少林武术爱好者的良师善友、得力助手。

是为序。

2015年6月5日

Preface

By Kou Wujiang[1]

Due to a work visit to the Shaolin Temple Wushu Training Center with my colleagues, Hongbo asked me after I watched their kungfu performance and training to provide a preface to the textbook that they were preparing to publish about Shaolin martial arts. Frankly speaking, I know little about martial arts forms and combat techniques, although I did spend some time researching martial arts culture and tourism. However, considering that the textbook would bring significant benefits not only for Shaolin cultural heritage but also for students of martial arts, I said yes.

Shaolin Martial Arts is a recognized brand for Henan cultural tourism and it enjoys a great reputation around the world. Since the Northern Wei Dynasty, Shaolin martial arts, along with Shaolin Zen culture, has been developed for more than 1,500 years. A rich and profound cultural tradition was nurtured and cultivated during this period. During the 80's of the last century, the China National Tourism Administration and the People's Government of Henan province built the Shaolin Temple Wushu Training Center based on a cultural philosophy of the Shaolin Temple, "The martial arts are recognized by the fame of the Shaolin Temple and the Temple is recognized by martial arts." The Shaolin Wushu Training Center was envisioned to play a key role in China's central region tourism project for spreading Henan's culture and meeting the peoples' desire to practice Shaolin Kungfu and watch Kungfu performances. Since 1988, the Wushu Center has carried out international communications and undertaken teaching activities based upon martial arts. Millions of tourists have been

---

[1] Kou Wujiang: Director General of Henan Provincial Tourism Administration.

attracted to visit the center and experience martial arts through specialized Shaolin tourism. Moreover, a large number of high level martial arts masters have been trained here. The center has made great contributions to the promotion of Shaolin martial arts as well as Henan's sustainable tourism development.

The Shaolin Temple has seen destruction several times in its history and Shaolin martial arts has also encountered challenges, even to the point of almost suffering extinction. In the 80's of the last century, our nation paid great attention to traditional martial arts culture, to systematically excavate and preserve the martial arts materials derived from prominent Shaolin monks and folk Kungfu masters. The materials were published through different methods to develop and promote Shaolin martial arts more effectively. However, published textbooks with an emphasis on teaching are rarely seen.

The Shaolin Temple Wushu Training Center has gathered many Shaolin Wushu masters and professionals who have devoted themselves in the long run to Shaolin martial arts culture research as well as to ensure that the research results can be put into practice; as well as continuous efforts of revising the technical theories and applications in the traditional practice sets. This textbook is the product of the accumulation of their research results in Shaolin wushu culture and the working experience through their performance, teaching and exchange over two decades. I believe that after this texbook is published, it will serve as an excellent reference to the people in the industry and to the general public who are interested in practicing Shaolin wushu.

The above serves as a foreword.

June 05, 2015

前 言

焦红波[①]

少林武术是中国宝贵的文化遗产,是武林中的一颗璀璨明珠。它内容广博,种类繁多,技法精湛,享誉中外。习练少林武术,不仅可以强健筋骨,防身抗暴,还可以陶冶情操,祛病延年。少林武术内静外猛、朴实无华、刚柔相济、立足实战,现已发展成为海内外广为流传的健身运动之一。

少林武术因发源于嵩山少林寺而得名。千百年来,作为少林武术发祥地的少林寺,因闻名天下的少林功夫和禅宗祖庭而被誉为"天下第一名刹"。地处少林寺的登封,因少林武术运动开展得非常广泛,也被称为"武术之乡"。为了传承与弘扬博大精深的少林武术,使少林武术以更大的步伐走向世界,1988年,作为向海内外传授少林武术基地的嵩山少林寺武术馆在少林武术发祥地诞生了。

河南省嵩山少林寺武术馆自创办之后,中外少林武术爱好者闻讯而至,习武练功。到目前为止,嵩山少林寺武术馆已培养了世界100多个国家和地区的武术学员2万余人。武馆自建立以来还为数以千万计的中外来宾展示精湛的少林武术。同时,嵩山少林寺武术馆还应邀到世界80多个国家和地区传授少林武术,使之在世界上生根、开花、结果。

嵩山少林寺武术馆由于地处少林武术发祥地和武术之乡的优势,汇集了众多少林武术高手在此传武研武,可谓人才济济。自建馆起,武术馆在传授少林武术的同时,还不断对少林武术进行深入的研究、挖掘和整理,并编写了许多具有代表性的少林武术文化书籍,为少林武术的传播和光大起到了重要的作用。

当前,在传习少林武术的过程中,系统、规范的少林武术教材的缺失致使少林武术在传播过程中出现诸多对其曲解和误解的现象。嵩山少林寺武

[①] 焦红波:河南省嵩山少林寺武术馆馆长、总教练,本书主编。

术馆作为国家建立的传播、弘扬和研究少林武术的中心，有责任、有义务编写一部权威性的介绍少林武术的书籍，以便为人们系统和完整学习少林武术提供强有力的保障。

本次编写的少林武术教材内容分为少林武术概论、少林武术基本动作和少林武术基本套路三部分。全书系统论述和介绍了少林武术的理论和具体习练方法，是学习和研究少林武术的必备之教材。本书按照少林武术一至九段的评位要求，分初级、中级、高级三个阶段，选取了少林十八势、少林烧火棍、少林长拳、七星拳、八段锦、易筋经等作为练习的功法，从而为求取段位者顺利通过段位的考核提供最有效的途径。特别要提出的是，本书中的部分内容，是我们与国家体委武术挖掘小组和北京体育大学门惠丰教授于 20 世纪 80 年代初共同创编的，经过多年的教学实践反映良好。

少林武术历史悠久，技法精湛，内容博大，需要探索和研究的还很多。因而在编写少林武术书籍之时，编写人员虽竭尽全力，但书中不当之处也再所难免，敬希各位方家及广大武术爱好者不吝赐教，以使其日臻完善。

2016 年 8 月 20 日

Foreword

By Jiao Hongbo[1]

Shaolin martial arts is a bright pearl and the precious cultural heritage of China. It enjoys enormous popularity throughout the world for its broad content, variety of types and exquisite techniques. Practicing martial arts can not only strengthen the muscles and bones, but also cultivate sentiments and keep healthy. Now it has become a popular worldwide sport due to its graceful and powerful movements, internal static, external fierce and actual combat experiences.

Shaolin martial arts originated from the Shaolin Temple, hence the name. It was reputed as the "No. 1 Temple under Heaven". Dengfeng city, where the Shaolin Temple was located, was renowned as the "Hometown of Chinese Kungfu" for the popular participation. In 1988, the Shaolin Temple Wushu Training Center was founded in Shaolin Village, its purpose is to inherit and carry forward the extensive and profound Shaolin martial arts.

Numerous enthusiasts of Shaolin Kungfu both in China and abroad practiced here, up to now, more than 20,000 students from over 100 countries and regions have been trained in this center. Tens of millions of visitors have enjoyed the consummate Kungfu shows since the establishment of the Wushu Training Center. Meanwhile professional coaches from this center have been invited to visit over 80 countries and regions to teach and impart Shaolin skills.

The Shaolin Temple Wushu Training Center is just located in the birthplace of Shaolin martial arts and the "Hometown of Chinese Kungfu", so numerous Kungfu masters gathered in this Training Center to study and practice. After cou-

---

[1] Jiao Hongbo: Director, Chief Coach of Shaolin Temple Wushu Training Center, Mt. Songshan, Henan Province.

ple of years of in-depth research, exploration and collecting, the Training Center composed a number of representative books which played an important role in promotion and popularity of Shaolin martial arts.

Systematic, standard and practical textbook is needed in order to avoid the phenomenon of misunderstanding and misinterpreting the discipline of Kungfu practices. As the state-level teaching base, the Shaolin Temple Wushu Training Center has the responsibility to compile this authoritative book to provide standard practices.

This Shaolin martial arts textbook consists of three parts: Introduction to Shaolin Martial Arts, Basic Shaolin Boxing Routines, and Basic Skills and Movements of Shaolin Martial Arts. The book, indispensable for studying Shaolin martial arts, describes systematically the theory and methods of Shaolin martial arts. Based on the requirements of Chinese martial arts Duan Ranking System from 1 to 9, the book describes selected Shaolin 18 Forms, Shaolin Shaohuo Stick, Shaolin Long Boxing, Shaolin Seven-star Boxing, Eight-sectioned Exercise(Baduanjin) and Channel-changing Scriptures(Yijinjing) as primary, middle and higher Dan(Rank) practicing routines, to make people who want to get higher grading in the examination have efficient way. It is necessary to be pointed out additionally that some parts of the textbook were completed with the cooperation of the martial arts research and exploration group of National Sports Commission and Professor Men Huifeng of Beijing Sports University in the early 1980s. The parts had produced notable effect by over years teaching practice.

Shaolin martial arts has a long history, consummate techniques, rich content which must be continually explored and studied. We have tried our best to finish this book, but we are still afraid there are some places that need to be perfected, so comments and suggestions will be greatly appreciated.

August 20th, 2016

目 录
CONTENT

第一章　少林大洪拳
Chapter 1　Shaolin Dahong Boxing ················ 1
　　第一节　套路动作名称
　　Quarter 1　Routine Name ················ 1
　　第二节　套路动作图解
　　Quarter 2　Figures of Routine Movements ················ 3

第二章　少林罗汉拳
Chapter 2　Shaolin Arhat Boxing ················ 41
　　第一节　套路动作名称
　　Quarter 1　Routine Name ················ 41
　　第二节　套路动作图解
　　Quarter 2　Figures of Routine Movements ················ 43

第三章　少林长拳
Chapter 3　Shaolin Long Boxing ················ 96
　　第一节　套路动作名称
　　Quarter 1　Routine Name ················ 96
　　第二节　套路动作图解
　　Quarter 2　Figures of Routine Movements ················ 98

第四章　少林七星拳
Chapter 4　Shaolin Seven-star Boxing ················ 128
　　第一节　套路动作名称
　　Quarter 1　Routine Name ················ 128

第二节　套路动作图解
Quarter 2　Figures of Routine Movements ………………………… 130

第五章　少林单刀
Chapter 5　Shaolin Single Broadsword ………………… 167
第一节　套路动作名称
Quarter 1　Routine Name ……………………………………………… 167
第二节　套路动作图解
Quarter 2　Figures of Routine Movements ………………………… 169

第六章　少林十三枪
Chapter 6　Shaolin 13-Spear ………………………………… 217
第一节　套路动作名称
Quarter 1　Routine Name ……………………………………………… 217
第二节　动作说明
Quarter 2　Movement Descriptions ………………………………… 218

第一章　少林大洪拳
Chapter 1　Shaolin Dahong Boxing

第一节　套路动作名称
Quarter 1　Routine Name

第一段
Section 1

1. 预备势（Preparation）
2. 白云盖顶（Overhead parrying）
3. 双云顶（Double overhead parrying）
4. 双震脚（Double stamping）
5. 七星架（Seven-star parrying）
6. 单鞭势（Single whipping posture）
7. 仆步切掌（Drop stance cutting）
8. 二起脚三抢手（Double kicking and triple grabbing）
9. 弓步顶肘（Bow stance elbowing）
10. 翻身压掌（Turning and palm pressing）
11. 迎面撒（Head-on spreading）

第二段
Section 2

12. 怀中抱月（Holding moon in arms）

13. 弓步推掌（Bow stance pushing）

14. 卧枕势（Pillowing lying gesture）

15. 前扫腿（Forward sweeping leg）

16. 金刚捣臼（Warrior's pounding）

17. 提手炮（Hand lifting cannon）

18. 古树盘根（Ancient tree rooting）

19. 三出手（Triple hand striking）

20. 海底炮（Punching downward）

21. 冲天炮（Punching upward）

22. 束身势（Restraining posture）

23. 双格锤（Double horizontal punching）

24. 双撅手（Double hand turning）

第三段

Section 3

25. 外摆腿（Leg swinging outward）

26. 打虎势（Tiger beating posture）

27. 盘肘（Elbow coiling）

28. 三抢手（Triple grabbing）

29. 箭弹抢手（Swift grabbing）

30. 回头望月（Back leg kicking）

31. 三扒手（Triple scratching）

32. 双震脚（Double stamping）

33. 虎抱头（Holding head with arms）

34. 弓步摆拳（Swing fist in bow stance）

35. 十字拍脚（Crossing slapping on leg）

36. 二起脚（Double kicking）

37. 坐山势（Mountain-like sitting）

38. 收势（Closing form）

第二节　套路动作图解
Quarter 2　Figures of Routine Movements

第一段
Section 1

1.预备势

(1)并步站立,成立正姿势,两臂自然下垂于体侧。目视前方(图1-1)。

1.Preparation

(1)Step touch, stand at attention, arms fall naturally on both sides. Look straight ahead (Figure 1-1).

图 1-1(Figure 1-1)

(2)两掌变拳抱于腰间。目视前方(图1-2)。

(2)Change palms into fists against the waist. Look straight ahead (Figure 1-2).

图 1-2(Figure 1-2)

2.白云盖顶

左脚向左开步,身体左转成左弓步;同时,左拳由腰间变掌架于头前上方,掌心斜向上。目视前方(图1-3)。

2.Overhead parrying

Left foot strides a step leftward, turn left into left bow stance; at the same time, change left fist at the waist into palm to parry overhead, palm center obliquely upward. Look straight ahead (Figure 1-3).

图 1-3(Figure 1-3)

3.双云顶

身体右转180°,左脚尖内扣,右脚尖外展,两腿弯曲;同时,左掌随身体向右、向后、向左,经头顶向下至腹前变拳,拳心向上;右拳变掌随左掌经胸前向右、向后、向左,经头顶向下至头部右上方变拳,拳心向下。目视右前方(图1-4)。

3.Double overhead parrying

Turn right 180°, left tiptoe buckles inward, right tiptoe stretch outward, bend legs; at the same time, swing left palm rightward, backward, leftward, over the head, forward to the front of the chest into fist, change right fist into palm, follow the left palm to swing rightward, backward, leftward, over the head, forward into fist at the top right of the head, fist center downward. Look right forward (Figure 1-4).

图 1-4(Figure 1-4)

4.双震脚

左右脚依次向身体中间靠拢震脚,两膝微屈下蹲;同时,右掌变拳,右小臂外旋、屈肘,以小臂外侧为力点向身体右侧施压,掌心向上;左掌变拳收至腹前,拳心向上。目视右前方(图1-5)。

4.Double stamping

Close left and right feet to the middle one another and stamp, bend knees slightly and squat; at the same time, change right palm into fist, bend and rotate right forearm outward to press down to the right side by taking the outside of forearm as a support, supinely; change left palm into fist to the front of the abdomen, fist center upward. Look right forward (Figure 1-5).

图 1-5(Figure 1-5)

5.七星架

右脚向前跨一步,左脚随之跟进在右脚内侧,脚尖点地,两腿屈膝半蹲成左丁步;同时,两小臂均内旋,左拳面顶住右拳腕内侧,以腰发力,向右前方冲拳,两拳心向下,与肩同高,目视正前方(图1-6)。

5.Seven-star parrying

Right foot strides forward, left foot follows to the inner side of right foot, tiptoes touchdown, bend knees on semi-crouch balance into left T-stance; at the same time, rotate both forearms inward, left fist face against the inner side of right wrist, deliver force with the waist to punch right forward, palm centers downward at the shoulders' level. Look straight ahead (Figure 1-6).

图 1-6(Figure 1-6)

6.单鞭势

(1)左脚向后撤一步,身体左转,两腿屈膝下蹲成马步;同时,两小臂外旋屈肘,两拳收到胸前,拳轮相对,拳心向内。目视正前方(图1-7)。

6.Single whipping posture

(1) Retreat left foot a step, turn left, bend legs to squat into horse riding stance; at the same time, rotate forearms outward with bending elbows, close fists to the front of the chest, palm center reverse sides face against each other. Look straight ahead (Figure 1-7).

图 1-7(Figure 1-7)

(2)上动不停,身体左转90°,左腿屈膝前弓,右腿蹬直成左弓步;同时,两拳经胸前分,向前、后两侧旋臂出拳,拳心向下,左臂略高于右臂。目视左拳(图1-8)。

(2) Keep moving, turn left 90°, bend left knee, keep right leg straight into left bow stance; at the same time, rotate fists inward separately to the front and back sides via the front of the chest, fist center downward, left arm is little higher than the right arm. Look at left fist (Figure 1-8).

图 1-8(Figure 1-8)

7.仆步切掌

(1)身体重心前移到左腿,右腿提膝;同时,左拳变掌向下、向右置腹前;右拳向下、向左置腹前,左掌拍击右拳上提于右臂上方。目视右拳(图1-9)。

7. Drop stance cutting

(1) Shift gravity center forward to left leg, raise right knee; at the same time, change left fist into palm downward, rightward to the front of the abdomen; right fist downward, leftward to the front of the abdomen, slap left palm against the back of right fist, lift it over right arm. Look at right fist (Figure 1-9).

图 1-9(Figure 1-9)

(2)上动不停,左脚蹬地跳起,右脚向左下方落地,左脚提起;同时,右拳收抱腰间,左掌回收置于右拳上。目视前下方(图1-10)。

(2) Keep moving, jump with left foot, right foot falls leftward on the ground, raise left foot; at the same time, close right fist against the waist, close

left palm on the right fist. Look front downward (Figure 1-10).

图 1-10(Figure 1-10)

(3)上动不停,左脚向左下方铲出成仆步;左掌随左脚同时向下切出,右拳收抱腰间。目视左前下方(图 1-11)。

(3) Keep moving, left foot shovels leftward into drop stance; left palm cuts down simultaneously following the left foot, close right fist against the waist. Look at left front downward (Figure 1-11).

图 1-11(Figure 1-11)

8.二起脚三抢手

(1)身体上起,右腿向前上一步成弓步;同时,左掌向前、向左经左脚面向上收于腰间抱拳。目视前方(图 1-12)。

8.Double kicking and triple grabbing

(1) Arise, right leg strides one step forward into bow stance; at the same time, swing left palm forward, leftward, close to the waist into fist via left instep. Look straight ahead (Figure 1-12).

图 1-12 (Figure 1-12)

(2)上动不停,左腿向前屈膝上摆,右腿蹬地腾空跳起向前上方弹踢,右拳由腰间变掌向前拍击右脚面。目视前方(图1-13)。

(2) Keep moving, swing left leg upward with bending knee, jump with right leg, right leg kicks upward, change right fist into palm at the waist to slap forward against right instep. Look straight ahead (Figure 1-13).

图 1-13(Figure 1-13)

(3)上动不停,身体下落右腿向前落步成右弓步;同时,右掌收至腰间由腰间再向前上方抢手,掌心向上,指尖向前与肩同高。目视右手指尖(图1-14)。

(3) Keep moving, right leg falls forward on the floor into right bow stance; at the same time, right hand has a sound slapping against the instep, closing to the waist, then grabs upward from the waist, supinely, fingertip forward at the level of shoulders. Look at right fingertip (Figure 1-14).

图 1-14 (Figure 1-14)

(4)上动不停,右掌变拳收抱腰间;同时,左拳由腰间变掌向前上方抢出。目视左掌(图1-15)。

(4) Keep moving. Change right palm into fist close to the waist; at the same time, change left palm into fist from the waist to grab upward. The requirement is as the same as above. Look at left palm (Figure 1-15).

图 1-15(Figure 1-15)

(5)上动不停,左掌变拳收抱腰间;同时,右拳由腰间变掌向前上方抢出。目视右掌(图1-16)。

(5)Keep moving, change left palm into fist close to the waist; at the same time, change right hand into palms at the waist to grab upward. The requirement is as the same as above. Look at right palm (Figure 1-16).

图 1-16(Figure 1-16)

9.弓步顶肘

(1)身体左转成弓步,右掌变拳屈肘,拳心向下,收至胸前;左拳变掌,按在右拳之上。目视右前方(图1-17)。

9.Bow stance elbowing

(1) Turn left into bow stance, change right hand into fist with bending elbow, fist center downward, closing to the front of the chest; change left hand into palm pressing on the right fist. Look right forward (Figure 1-17).

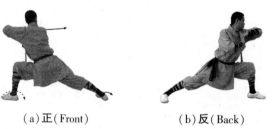

(a)正(Front)　　　　　(b)反(Back)

图 1-17(Figure 1-17)

(2)身体右转成右弓步;同时,以腰发力,右肘向前顶击,力达肘尖,肘与肩同高。目视右肘尖(图1-18)。

(2) Turn right into right bow stance; at the same time, exert force with the waist, right elbow pounds forward at the level of shoulders. Look at right elbow (Figure 1-18).

图 1-18(Figure 1-18)

10.翻身压掌

(1)身体重心移至左腿,右腿提膝;左掌变拳收抱腰间,右拳向下收抱腰间。目视右前方(图1-19)。

10. Turning and palm pressing

(1) Shift gravity center to left leg, lift right knee; change left palm into fist against the waist, keep right fist in front of the chest. Look right forward (Figure 1-19).

图 1-19(Figure 1-19)

(2)上动不停,右脚落地,左脚随即提起跟进,落在右腿前,身体右转180°,下蹲成半马步,重心偏向右;同时,右拳向上、向右经头顶前上方向下,向右收抱腰间;左拳变掌从体侧向上、向右,经头顶上方向下按在左膝前,掌心向下。目视左掌(图1-20)。

(2) Keep moving, right foot falls, left foot follows to be lift and falls in

front of the right leg, turn right 180° and squat into half horse riding stance, gravity center rightward; at the same time, swing right palm upward, rightward, via the front of the head, downward, rightward, close to the waist; change left fist into palm, swinging upward, rightward, via the top of the head, to press downward in front of the left knee, palm center downward. Look at left palm (Figure 1- 20).

图 1-20(Figure 1- 20)

11.迎面撒

(1)身体重心前移,右腿蹬地成左弓步;同时,右拳变爪从腰间向身体左前下方按爪。目视右爪(图 1-21)。

11. Head-on spreading

(1) Gravity center forward, right leg stamps into left bow stance; at the same time, change right fist into claw to scratch left downward from the waist. Look at right claw (Figure 1-21).

图 1-21(Figure 1-21)

(2)上动不停,身体右转上起;同时,右爪变拳向右、向上屈肘置身体右侧与肩同高;在身体右转上起的同时,右脚向前一步震腿,左腿提膝。目视右拳(图 1-22)。

(2) Keep moving, turn right and arise; at the same time, change right claw into fist rightward, upward to bend elbow to the right side at the level of shoulders; as soon as turning right and arising, right foot strides a step forward

to stamp, lift left knee. Look at right fist (Figure 1-22).

图 1-22(Figure 1-22)

(3)上动不停,左腿向左前方落地成弓步;同时,右拳变掌由体侧向左前方推掌,五指分开,掌心向前。目视前方(图1-23)。

(3) Keep moving, left leg falls leftward into left bow stance; at the same time, push right palm left forward from the side, five fingers apart, palm center forward. Look straight ahead (Figure 1-23).

图 1-23(Figure 1-23)

第二段

Section 2

12.怀中抱月

(1)身体向右后转180°,右腿向左侧回收半步,脚尖点地成右虚步;右掌向下、向右至体前;左拳变掌,掌心向上抵于右上臂。目视右掌(图1-24)。

12. Holding moon in arms

(1) Turn right backward 180°, close right leg half a step leftward, tiptoe touchdown into right empty stance; swing right palm downward and then rightward to the front of the body, change left fist into palm, supinely against right

forearm. Look at right palm (Figure 1-24).

图 1-24（Figure 1-24）

（2）上动不停,右臂屈肘由掌变拳向上、向内、向下划弧;同时,左掌变拳向下、向前、向上,经右拳前上方绕至胸前;右拳向前上方摆至左拳前,左拳在内,两拳心均向下。目视右拳(图 1-25)。

(2) Keep moving, bend right arm to draw an arc upward, inward and downward; at the same time, change left palm into fist downward, forward, upward and over right fist to the front of the chest, swing left palm forward and upward to the front of left fist, left fist inside, both fist centers downward. Look at right fist (Figure 1-25).

图 1-25（Figure 1-25）

13. 弓步推掌

右脚向前迈半步成右弓步;同时,左拳向前、向下,经体前收至腰间;当左拳经右胸前时,右拳变掌由左拳上方向右前方推掌,掌尖向上与颏同高。目视右掌(图 1-26)。

13. Bow stance pushing

Right foot strides forward half a step into right bow stance; at the same time, left fist moves forward, downward to the waist via the front of the body; when left fist moves to the front of right chest, change right fist into palm to push right forward via over left fist, fingertips upward at the level of the chin. Look at right palm (Figure 1-26).

图 1-26(Figure 1-26)

14.卧枕势

(1)身体左转成左弓步;同时,右臂内旋由掌变拳向下、向左摆至体侧,拳心向后。目视前方(图 1-27)。

14. Pillowing lying gesture

(1) Turn left into left bow stance; at the same time, rotate right arm inward, change palm into fist to swing downward and leftward to the side, palm center backward. Look straight ahead (Figure 1-27).

图 1-27(Figure 1-27)

(2)上动不停,身体重心左移,身体右转,右腿向前提膝下落,左脚提起,身体重心在右腿;同时,右拳向左、向上、向右、向下,摆击至体侧胯旁,拳心向上;左拳由腰间向左、向上、向右、向下摆至左腹前,拳眼向上。目视左拳(图 1-28)。

(2) Keep moving, shift gravity center leftward, lift left foot slightly to fall forward, turn right; at the same time, swing right palm leftward, upward, rightward, downward and rightward to the hip, fist center upward; swing left fist from the waist leftward, upward, rightward and downward to the front of the left

abdomen, fist eye upward. Look at left fist (Figure 1-28).

图 1-28（Figure 1-28）

（3）上动不停，左脚向左落步，屈膝前弓成左弓步；同时，右拳向右、向上、向左、向下冲拳至裆前，拳心向右后；左拳向下，向右经腹前屈肘向上顶击至左肩前，拳心向内。目视右下方（图1-29）。

（3）Keep moving, left foot falls leftward, bend knee forward into left bow stance; at the same time, plunge right fist rightward, upward, leftward and downward to the front of the crotch, palm center rightward; left fist downward and rightward, bend elbow in front of the abdomen to hit upward to the front of the left shoulder, palm center inward. Look right downward (Figure 1-29).

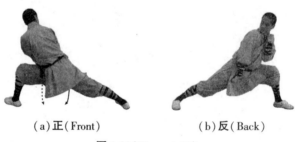

(a) 正 (Front)　　　　　(b) 反 (Back)

图 1-29（Figure 1-29）

15. 前扫腿

（1）身体下蹲，左腿屈膝，右腿伸直成仆步；两掌按于体前，两掌心向下。目视右前下方（图1-30）。

15. Forward sweeping leg

（1）Squat, right leg straight into right drop stance; press palms in front of the crotch, both fingertips right forward. Look at right front downward (Figure

1-30)。

图 1-30（Figure 1-30）

（2）右腿向前、向左扫转180°；当右腿经过体前时左掌抬起，随之下落按至体前，身体微向右前倾。目视左前下方（图1-31）。

(2) Right leg sweeps 180° forward and leftward; when right leg moves to the front of the body, lift palms, and then press them down in front of the body, which is obliquely forward. Look at left front downward (Figure 1-31).

图 1-31（Figure 1-31）

（3）上动不停，右腿继续向后扫转；左脚蹬地离地，而后落地，使右腿经左腿下向后，向右扫转成右仆步。目视右前下方（图1-32）。

(3) Keep moving, right leg continues sweeping backward; left foot jumps and falls after the right leg sweeps through, right leg sweeps continuously rightward into right drop stance. Look at right front downward (Figure 1-32).

图 1-32（Figure 1-32）

16.金刚捣臼

上动不停,身体上起,左腿屈膝前弓成左弓步;同时,左掌向上置于左膝上方,掌心向上;右拳向上、向左经头顶上方(身体左拧)向左前下方左掌心处捣臼,拳心向内(下砸锤);同时,以气催力,鼻音由口腔发"嗯"的声音。目视右拳(图1-33)。

16. Warrior's pounding

Keep moving, arise, bend left leg into front bow stance; at the same time, swing right palm upward and leftward to pound down via the front of the head (body twists leftward), palm center inward to strike in left palm center by the inside of left knee. Look at right fist; at the same time, shout by taking the advantage of the action. Look at right fist (Figure 1-33).

图1-33(Figure 1-33)

17.提手炮

右脚向前与左脚靠拢并震脚;同时,右拳向上撩打,左掌向前、向上、向后与右拳背在腹前相击(上撩锤);两腿微屈下蹲,借势从丹田发出"咦"的声音。目视右拳(图1-34)。

17. Hand lifting cannon

Close right foot forward to left foot and stamp; at the same time, right fist hits upward, left palm moves forward, upward and backward to hit against the right fist back in front of the lower abdomen; bend legs and squat, shout by taking the advantage of the action. Look at right fist (Figure 1-34).

(a)正(Front)　　(b)反(Back)

图 1-34(Figure 1-34)

18.古树盘根

右腿向右横跨一步,左脚随即跟进一步靠在右脚内侧,脚尖点地,两腿屈膝半蹲成左丁步;同时,右拳向右、向后置于身体后方,拳心向后;左掌变拳向右置于腹前右侧,拳心向内。目视左前下方(图 1-35)。

18. Ancient tree rooting

Right leg strides rightward a step, left foot follows to the inside of the right foot, tiptoe touchdown, bend knees on semi-crouch balance into left T step; at the same time, wave right fist rightward, backward and leftward to the back of the body, palm center backward; change left palm into fist to the right side of the abdomen, palm center inward. Look at left front downward(Figure 1-35).

(a)正(Front)　　(b)反(Back)

图 1-35(Figure 1-35)

19.三出手

(1)左腿向左迈步成左弓步;同时,两拳经体前向左侧撩击。左拳在上,拳眼向下;右拳在下,拳眼向上。目视左拳(图 1-36)。

19. Triple hand striking

(1) Left leg strides leftward into left bow stance; at the same time, fists strike upward and leftward via the front of the body. Left fist above, fist eye downward; right fist below, fist eye upward. Look at left fist (Figure 1-36).

图 1-36(Figure 1-36)

(2)身体右转成右弓步,两拳由左侧向下、向右,经腹前向右上方撩打。右拳在外,拳心向内;左拳在内,拳心向外。目视右拳(图1-37)。

(2) Turn right into right bow stance, fists moves downward and rightward from the left side to strike rightward and upward. Right fist outside, fist center inward; left fist inside, fist center outward. Look at right fist (Figure 1-37).

图 1-37(Figure 1-37)

(3)身体左转270°,右脚向前盖步;同时,两拳向上、向左,经头前上方向下,经腹前向身体左下方打出。左拳在上,右拳在下,两拳眼相对。目视左拳(图1-38)。

(3) Turn left 270°, right foot strides right forward; at the same time, fists

moves upward, leftward, via the front of the head, downward to strike leftward via the front of the abdomen. Left fist above, right fist below, fist centers against each other. Look at left fist (Figure 1-38).

图 1-38(Figure 1-38)

(4) 左腿从右腿后侧向右叉步,脚尖点地;同时,两拳向右经腹前向右上方打出,右拳在上,左拳在下,两拳眼向内。目视右拳(图1-39)。

(4) Left leg moves rightward from back of the right leg into cross stance, tiptoe touchdown; at the same time, fists strike right upward via the front of the abdomen, right fist above, left fist below, both fist eyes inward. Look at right fist (Figure 1-39).

图 1-39(Figure 1-39)

20.海底炮

(1)上体向左上方扭转翻身;同时,左拳向左、向上摆至头顶上方,右拳随转体摆至右胯外侧,拳心向外。目视左拳(图1-40)。

20. Punching downward

(1) Upper body turns left upward; at the same time, swing left fist leftward, upward over the head, right fist follows the turning of the body to swing to the outside of the right hip, both fist centers outward. Look at left fist (Fig-

ure 1-40).

图 1-40(Figure 1-40)

（2）上动不停,身体继续左转;右脚向前一步同左脚并拢后,屈膝双脚向下震脚,震脚时先右脚后左脚;同时,左拳向前、向下,屈肘向上经腹前摆到右胸前,拳心向内;右拳向上、向左、向下冲拳至两膝之间,左拳在内,右拳在外。目视右拳(图1-41)。

(2) Keep moving, go on turning left; lift right foot, falls on the right side of the left foot, feet together, bend knees and stamp with right foot first and the left then; at the same time, swing left palm forward and downward, and then upward with bending elbow to the front of the right chest via the front of the abdomen, palm center inward; punch right fist upward, leftward, then downward to the position between knees, left fist inside and right fist outside. Look at right fist (Figure 1-41).

图 1-41(Figure 1-41)

21.冲天炮

（1）身体上起,右脚抬起下落震脚,两脚靠拢,两膝微屈;同时,右拳屈肘,从左臂内侧向上冲拳,拳心向内与颏同高;左拳向下盖压横于腹前,拳眼向上,拳心向内。目视前方(图1-42)。

21. Punching upward

(1) Arise, lift right foot, falling and stamping, legs together, bend knees

slightly; at the same time, bend right elbow, punch right fist upward from the inside of the left arm, palm center inward at the chin's level; press left fist downward to the front of the abdomen, fist eye upward, fist center inward. Look straight ahead (Figure 1-42).

图 1-42(Figure 1-42)

（2）重心后移，左腿后退半步震脚，右脚尖点地；同时，左拳向上冲出与颏同高，拳心向内；右拳抱回腰间。目视左拳(图 1-43)。

(2) Shift gravity center backward, retreat left foot half a step with a stamp, right tiptoe touchdown; at the same time, punch left fist upward at the chin's level, fist center inward; close right fist against the waist. Look at left fist (Figure 1-43).

图 1-43(Figure 1-43)

（3）上动不停，重心后移，右脚后退一步震脚，左脚尖点地；同时，右拳由腰间向上冲出与颏同高，拳心向内；左拳抱至腰间。目视右拳(图 1-44)。

(3) Keep moving, shift gravity center backward, retreat right foot half a step with a stamp, left tiptoe touchdown; at the same time, punch right fist from the waist upward at the chin's level, fist center inward; close left fist against the waist. Look at right fist (Figure 1-44).

图 1-44(Figure 1-44)

22.束身势

身体右转,重心移向右腿,左脚收至右脚内侧,脚尖点地,两腿屈膝下蹲成左丁步;右拳至胸前,拳心向内;左拳向下冲于体侧,拳心向后。目视左前方(图1-45)。

22. Restraining posture

Turn right, shift gravity center to right leg, close left foot to the inside of the right foot, tiptoe touchdown, bend legs to squat into left T-step; right fist moves to the front of the chest, palm center inward; punch left fist downward to the side of the body, fist center leftward. Look left forward (Figure 1-45).

(a)正(Front)　　　　　(b)反(Back)

图 1-45(Figure 1-45)

23.双格锤

(1)身体左转,左脚向左迈步成左弓步;同时,腰向左拧,右拳由右胸前向前横击至体前,拳心向内;左拳收抱于腰间。目视右拳(图1-46)。

23. Double horizontal punching

(1) Turn left, left foot strides leftward into left bow stance; at the same time, waist twists leftward, punch right fist forward horizontally from the front of the right chest, fist center inward; close left fist against the waist. Look at the right fist (Figure 1-46).

图 1-46 (Figure 1-46)

(2) 上动不停,身体重心向前移至左腿,右腿向前提膝;同时,左拳由腰间向体前横击,拳心向内,拳眼向外;右拳收抱于腰间。目视左拳(图1-47)。

(2) Keep moving, shift gravity center forward, lift right knee and bend left knee; at the same time, punch left fist forward horizontally from the waist, fist center inward, fist eye outward; close right fist against the waist. Look at left fist (Figure 1-47).

图 1-47 (Figure 1-47)

(3) 上动不停,右脚向前落地,左脚随即跳步提起(跳换步);同时,左拳下压至腹前,拳心向内;右拳抱在腰间。目视左拳(图1-48)。

(3) Keep moving, right foot falls forward on the floor, lift left foot (inter-

changing jump); at the same time, left fist presses downward to the front of the abdomen, fist center inward, fist eye upward; close right fist against the waist. Look at left fist (Figure 1-48).

图 1-48(Figure 1-48)

24.双撅手

(1)左脚前落成左弓步;两拳变掌,左掌在前与胸同高,右掌在后向前置于腹前,两掌心均向上。目视左掌(图 1-49)。

24. Double hand turning

(1) Left foot falls forward on the floor into left bow stance; change fists into palms, left palm in front at the level of the chest, right palm behind to the front of the abdomen, both palm centers upward. Look at left palm (Figure 1-49).

图 1-49(Figure 1-49)

(2)右掌向前经左掌下方向上、向内、向下至胸前变拳,拳心向下;左掌向下、向前、向上经右掌前方上绕至胸前变拳,拳心向下置于右拳前(双撅手)。目视左拳(图 1-50)。

(2) Right palm moves forward, through under left palm, upward, inward to the front of the chest into fist, palm center downward; left palm

moves upward, forward and upward via the front of the right palm to the front of the chest into fist, fist center downward in front of the right fist. Look at left fist (Figure 1-50).

图 1-50 (Figure 1-50)

第三段

Section 3

25.外摆腿

(1) 身体右转180°,重心移到左腿上;两拳收抱于腰间。目视前方(图1-51)。

25. Leg swinging outward

(1) Turn right 180°, shift gravity center to the left leg; close fists against the waist, fist centers upward. Look straight ahead (Figure 1-51).

图 1-51 (Figure 1-51)

(2) 上动不停,两腿屈膝,右腿用力蹬地,使身体右转腾空,右腿向右上侧摆,左腿自然下垂;同时,两拳变掌,掌心向下,从腰间由右向左依次拍击右脚面。目视两掌(图1-52)。

(2) Keep moving, bend legs, swing left leg right upward, try hard to jump with right leg and turn right, swing left leg right upward; at the same time, change fists into palms, palm centers downward, to slap against right instep one another from right to left from the waist; left foot hangs naturally. Look at the hand (Figure 1-52).

图 1-52(Figure 1-52)

26.打虎势

左腿落地，右腿向右后方摆击下落成右弓步；同时，两掌变拳，右拳由胸前向右侧屈肘架于头顶上方；左拳由胸前向右下方屈臂盘肘，拳心向内。目视前方(图 1-53)。

26. Tiger beating posture

Left leg falls, swing right leg rightward and falls into right bow stance; at the same time, change palms into fists, swing right fist to the right side from the front of the chest, then upward to parry overhead with bending elbow, plunge left fist right downward to the front of the right abdomen from the front of the chest, fist center inward. Look forward (Figure 1-53).

图 1-53(Figure 1-53)

27.盘肘

身体左转成左弓步;同时,左拳向下、向左、向上划弧架于头顶上方,拳心向上;右臂屈肘下落,由右向前、向左盘肘,拳面抵胸口,肘尖向前;上身左拧。目视前方(图1-54)。

27. Elbow coiling

Turn left into left bow stance; at the same time, left fist draws an arc downward, leftward, then upward to parry in front of the forehead, fist center upward; right arm falls with bending elbow, coil elbow from right to the front and left when right arm falls with bending elbow, fist face against the chest, elbow tip forward; upper body twists rightward. Look straight ahead (Figure 1-54).

图 1-54(Figure 1-54)

28.三抢手

(1)右脚向前上一步成右弓步;同时,左拳内旋下压经体前收至腰间;当左拳经右胸前时,右拳变掌由左拳上方向前抢手(插掌),掌心向上,指尖向前。目视右掌(图1-55)。

28. Triple grabbing

(1) Right foot strides forward into right bow stance; at the same time, rotate left fist inward to press down, close it against the waist via the front of the body, at this moment, change right fist into palm to grab (thrust) forward via left palm center, supinely, finger tips forward. Look at right palm (Figure 1-55).

图1-55(Figure 1-55)

(2)上动不停,左脚向前上一步成左弓步;同时,右掌变拳收抱腰间,左拳变掌经右拳上方向前抢手(插掌),掌心向上,指尖向前。目视左掌(图1-56)。

(2) Keep moving, left foot advances a step into left bow stance; at the same time, change right hand into fist to the waist, change left fist into palm to grab (thrust) via right fist center, supinely, finger tips forward. Look at left palm (Figure 1-56).

图1-56(Figure 1-56)

(3)上动不停,右脚向前上一步,左腿随即跟进向前上方弹腿;同时,左手变拳抱回腰间;右拳变掌经左掌上方向前内旋抢手(插掌),掌心向上,指尖向前。目视右抢手(图1-57)。

(3) Keep moving, right leg advances a step forward, bend knee, left leg follows immediately, lift knee; at the same time, change left hand into fist to the waist; change right fist into palm to turn upward via the left fist center, rotate forearm inward to grab (thrust), supinely, finger tips forward. Look at right grabbing hand (Figure 1-57).

图 1-57（Figure 1-57）

29.箭弹抢手

上动不停,右脚蹬地,身体腾空,右腿快速向上弹踢,脚面绷直,左腿自然下垂;同时,右掌外旋收至腰间,左拳变掌经右掌上方向前抢出,掌心向上。目视左掌(图 1-58)。

29. Swift grabbing

Keep moving, jump with right foot, right leg kicks quickly upward, keeping instep straight, left leg hangs naturally; at the same time, rotate right palm outward to the waist, change left fist into palm to thrust upward via right palm center, supinely. Look at left palm (Figure 1-58).

图 1-58（Figure 1-58）

30.回头望月

左脚落地,身体右转 90°,右脚向右后下方落步成右弓步;同时,左小臂内旋,左掌收置胸前变爪由下经腹前向身体左侧下按,爪心斜向下;右掌掌心向下,向前经左小臂下方穿出,再内旋向上、向右至额斜上方,内旋架掌。目视左前方(图 1-59)。

30. Back leg kicking

Left foot falls on the ground, turn right 90°, retreat right foot right backward into right bow stance; at the same time, rotate left forearm inward, close left hand to the front of the chest, change it into claw to press right downward via the front of lower abdomen, claw center downward; make right palm center downward to thrust out under the left forearm, then to rotate inward, upward and then rightward over the forehead, parry it with inward rotating. Look left forward (Figure 1-59).

图 1-59（Figure 1-59）

31.三扒手

（1）左腿经右腿后方向左插步，身体下蹲成歇步；同时，左掌向上、向右至腹前；右掌向下、向左，右拇指与左拇指相扣，掌心向外。目视右前方（图1-60）。

31. Triple scratching

(1) Insert left leg rightward behind the left leg, squat into right sitting stance; at the same time, left palm moves upward, rightward to the front of the right abdomen; right palm downward, leftward, buckle right thumb and left thumb together, palm centers outward. Look right forward (Figure 1-60).

图 1-60（Figure 1-60）

（2）上动不停，右脚向右一步，身体下蹲成马步；同时，两掌向左、向上划弧至左胸前，掌心向外。目视两掌（图1-61）。

(2) Keep moving, right foot strides rightward a step, squat into horse

riding stance; at the same time, palms draw an arc leftward, upward to the front of the left chest, palm center outward. Look at palms (Figure 1-61).

图 1-61(Figure 1-61)

（3）上动不停,左腿经右腿后方向右插步,身体下蹲成歇步;同时,两掌向右、向下划弧至腹前,保持互扣,掌心向外。目视右前方(图 1-62)。

(3) Keep moving, left leg inserts rightward behind the right leg, squat into sitting stance; at the same time, palms draw an arc rightward, downward to the front of the abdomen, keeping buckling each other, palm centers outward. Look right forward (Figure 1-62).

图 1-62(Figure 1-62)

（4）紧接上动,身体上起,右腿提膝;同时,两掌保持相扣,向左、向上划弧至左胸前,掌心向外。目视左前方(图 1-63)。

(4) Continuously, stand up, lift right knee; at the same time, keep palms buckling each other, palms draw an arc leftward, upward to the front of left chest, palm center outward. Look left forward (Figure 1-63).

图 1-63（Figure 1-63）

32.双震脚

两掌由左向右、向上划弧至腹前时,两掌变拳,收抱腰间,拳心向上;同时,右脚落地,与左脚并步向下震脚。目视右前方(图1-64)。

32. Double stamping

Palms draw an arc leftward, rightward, upward from the left to the front of the abdomen, change palms into fists to the waist, supinely; at the same time, right foot falls, close to the left foot with a stamp. Look right forward (Figure 1-64).

图 1-64（Figure 1-64）

33.虎抱头

右脚向右一步,左脚随即跟进脚尖点地靠在右脚内侧,身体下蹲成左丁步;同时,右拳向右、向下、向上架于头顶上方,拳心向上;左拳经腹前向右横击至腹右侧,拳心向内。目视左前方(图1-65)。

33. Holding head with arms

Right foot strides rightward a step, left foot follows at once close to the inside of right foot, tiptoe touchdown touch, squat into left T-step; at the same

34

time, swing right fist rightward, downward, upward to parry overhead, fist center upward; swing left fist to the right side horizontally via the front of the abdomen, fist center inward. Look left forward (Figure 1-65).

图 1-65(Figure 1-65)

34.弓步摆拳

左脚向左一步,左腿前弓成左弓步;同时,右拳由上向下收抱腰间;左拳由右腹前向右横击于体侧,肘贴左肋,拳心向上。目视前方(图1-66)。

34. Swing fist in bow stance

Left foot strides leftward, bend left leg forward into left bow stance; at the same time, close right fist up-down against the waist; swing left fist horizontally to the left side from the front of right abdomen, elbow against left ribs, fist center upward. Look straight ahead (Figure 1-66).

图 1-66(Figure 1-66)

35.十字拍脚

(1)右脚向前上一步;同时,左拳收至腰间。目视前方(图1-67)。

35. Crossing slapping against on leg

(1) Right foot advances a step; at the same time, close left fist against the

waist. Look straight ahead (Figure 1-67).

图 1-67(Figure 1-67)

（2）上动不停，重心移至右腿，左腿向前上方弹踢，脚面绷直；同时，右拳变掌，由腰间向前插掌，迅速拍击左脚面。目视前方（图1-68）。

(2) Keep moving, change gravity center to right leg, left leg kicks up forward, keeping instep straight; at the same time, change right fist into palm to thrust forward from the waist, turn palm in front of the chest, palm center downward, to slap against left instep immediately. Look straight ahead (Figure 1-68).

图 1-68(Figure 1-68)

（3）上动不停，左脚向前落步；同时，右掌变拳收抱腰间。目视前方（图1-69）。

(3) Keep moving, after sounding slapping, left foot falls forward at once into bow stance; at the same time, change right palm into fist to the waist. Look straight ahead (Figure 1-69).

第一章　少林大洪拳

图 1-69（Figure 1-69）

（4）上动不停,右腿向前、向上弹踢,脚面绷直;同时,左拳变掌由腰间向前插掌,迅速拍击右脚面。目视前方(图 1-70)。

（4）Keep moving, right leg kicks up forward, keeping instep straight; at the same time, change left fist into palm to thrust forward from the waist, turn palm in front of the chest, palm center downward, to slap against right instep immediately. Look straight ahead（Figure 1-70）.

图 1-70（Figure 1-70）

36.二起脚

（1）右脚向前落步,左掌变拳收抱腰间。目视前方(图 1-71)。

36. Double kicking

（1）Right foot falls forward, rotate left palm outward into fist to the waist. Look straight ahead（Figure 1-71）.

37

图 1-71（Figure 1-71）

（2）身体重心移至右腿，右腿蹬地跳起，身体腾空；右腿向前上方摆，脚面绷直，左腿自然下垂；右拳变掌由腰间向前插出，在胸前翻掌，迅速迎击右脚面。目视前方（图 1-72）。

(2) Shift gravity center to right leg, jump with right leg, bend left leg to swing upward; swing right leg up forward, keep instep straight, left leg hangs naturally; change right fist into palm to thrust forward from the waist, turn palm in front of the chest to slap against right instep immediately. Look straight ahead (Figure 1-72).

图 1-72（Figure 1-72）

37.坐山势

（1）左脚落地，身体右转 90°，随即右脚下落震脚，左腿提膝，右掌变拳随右腿下落转体之势向下、向右划弧于身体右侧，拳心向内，拳眼向上；左拳同时向上摆击于左肩上方，拳心向内，拳眼向下。目视左拳（图 1-73）。

37. Mountain-like sitting

(1) Left foot falls on the floor, turn right 90°, immediately right foot falls with a stamp, raise left knee, change right palm into fist to draw a arc downward

and rightward to the right side when turning and falling, fist center inward; at the same time, punch left fist upward to the left shoulder, fist center inward. Look at left fist (Figure 1-73).

图 1-73（Figure 1-73）

（2）上动不停，左脚向左侧落步屈膝下蹲成马步；右拳向上、向左摆击上架于头前上方；左拳下栽于左膝上，左臂微屈外展；头随右拳上摆的同时左摆。以气催力发出"威"的声音。目视左前方（图1-74）。

(2) Keep moving. Left foot strides leftward into horse riding stance; swing right palm upward and leftward to parry overhead; plunge left fist downward on the left knee, bend left arm slightly to stretch outward; head sways leftward immediately when swinging right palm upward. Look left forward and make a sound of "wei" at the same time (Figure 1-74).

图 1-74（Figure 1-74）

38.收势

（1）左脚向右收步，两脚并拢，身体直立；两拳收于腰间成抱拳势。目视前方（图1-75）。

38. Closing form

(1) Close left foot to right foot, step touch, stand upright, close fists against the waist. Look straight ahead (Figure 1-75).

图 1-75(Figure 1-75)

(2)两拳变掌,两臂伸直下垂于身体两侧,成立正姿势。目视前方(图 1-76)。

(2) Change fists into palms, arms straight and hang against both sides into standing at attention. Look straight ahead (Figure 1-76).

图 1-76(Figure 1-76)

第二章　少林罗汉拳
Chapter 2　Shaolin Arhat Boxing

第一节　套路动作名称
Quarter 1　Routine Name

第一段
Section 1

1. 预备势（Preparation）
2. 童子拜佛（Boy worshipping the Buddha）
3. 马步双推掌（Horse-riding pushing palms）
4. 蹲桩捶（Piling punch）
5. 单叉（Single fork）
6. 怀中抱月（Holding moon in arms）
7. 仆步切掌（Bend and cut palm）
8. 弓步冲拳（Keep legs still and punching）
9. 转身背后捶（Turning punch）

第二段
Section 2

10. 架起捶（Parrying fist）
11. 转身斜劈掌（Turning and chopping palm）
12. 提鞋蹬腿（Lifting and kicking）

13.倒步连三掌（Retreating and repeated chopping）

14.转身夯地捶（Turning and ramming）

15.撑臂后蹬腿（Extending retreating and kicking）

16.劈腿卧地捶（Lying and chopping）

17.右转拉弓势（Rightward turning and bow pulling）

18.转身底手炮（Turning and punching）

第三段

Section 3

19.坐山势（Mountain riding）

20.抖毛（Shaking hair）

21.左转上步一拳（Leftward turning and punching）

22.转身弹腿推掌（Turning and kicking）

23.转身飞里拔腿（Turning and kicking in the air）

24.撞金钟（Bell punching）

25.转身双冲肘（Turning and double punching）

26.上步抢手（Step advancing and palming）

27.蹲桩捶（Piling punch）

第四段

Section 4

28.卧枕势（Sleeping and punching）

29.老僧拔葱（Sudden jumping）

30.蹲伸播种（Squatting and stretching）

31.提鞋后蹬腿（Backward turning and kicking）

32.二起脚（Double kicking）

33.束身双摆掌（Closing and double swinging）

34.里扫堂腿（Sweeping and kicking）

35.老僧照镜（Mirroring）

36.伏身摸瓜（Bending and searching）

37.迎面撒（Head-on sweeping）

38.老僧端锅（Holding and fetching）

39.跳起弹踢(Jumping and kicking)

40.双抢手(Double grabbing)

41.转身罗汉眉(Turning Arhat eyebrow)

42.双展翅(Turning swinging)

43.双架棚(Double parrying)

44.五子登科(Jumping and soaring)

45.坐山势(Mountain riding)

46.收势(Closing)

第二节　套路动作图解

Quarter 2　Figures of Routine Movements

第一段

Section 1

1.预备势

(1)两脚并立,两臂自然下垂于身体两侧,挺胸收腹,成立正姿势。目视前方(图2-1)。

1.Preparation

(1)Feet parallel, arms fall naturally, stand at attention. Look straight ahead (Figure 2-1).

图2-1(Figure 2-1)

(2)两臂屈肘向上提,两掌变拳抱于腰间;同时,左脚向左一步,与肩同宽。目视前方(图2-2)。

(2) Bend elbows upward, change palms into fists against the waist, at the same time, left foot strides one step leftward, the same wide as the shoulders. Look straight ahead (Figure 2-2).

图 2-2(Figure 2-2)

2.童子拜佛

右腿屈膝半蹲,左腿屈膝提起盘放在右膝上;同时,两拳变掌合掌向上收于胸前,指尖向上。目视前方(图2-3)。

2.Boy worshipping the Buddha

Bend right knee on semi-crouch balance, bend and lift left knee on the right knee, at the same time, put palms together in front of the chest, fingertips upward. Look straight ahead (Figure 2-3).

图 2-3(Figure 2-3)

3.马步双推掌

左脚向左侧落步成马步;同时,两掌分别向左右推出,成立掌。目视左前方(图 2-4)。

3.Horse-riding pushing palms

Left foot strides leftward and falls into the horse-riding stance, at the same time, push palms leftward and rightward into raised palms. Look left forward (Figure 2-4).

图 2-4(Figure 2-4)

4.蹲桩捶

(1)左脚以脚跟为轴,右脚以脚掌为轴,向左转体,重心移向左脚;同时,左手拇指分开,虎口张大,右臂内旋,掌心向下。目视左手方向(图 2-5)。

4.Piling punch

(1) Turn left with the left heel and right sole as the axis, shift gravity center to left foot, at the same time, the left thumb apart and the part between the thumb and the forefinger expanded, the right arm turns inward, palm center downward. Look at left hand (Figure 2-5).

图 2-5(Figure 2-5)

(2)紧接上动,左臂外旋屈肘,左掌变拳,拳心向里。右掌变拳下落,拳眼向上。目视左手方向(图 2-6)。

(2) Left arm rotates outward bend the elbow, change left palm into fist, palm center inward. Change right palm into fist and fall, eye of fist upward. Look at left hand (Figure 2-6).

图 2-6(Figure 2-6)

(3)上动不停,右脚向前跟步,向左脚并拢,两腿屈膝半蹲;右拳由下向前勾拳,右臂微屈,拳面向上,拳与肩同高;同时,左拳向下置于右肘下方。目视前方(图 2-7)。

(3) Keep moving, right foot forward, close it to left foot, bend knees on semi-crouch balance, swing right fist forward into a hook, bend right arm slightly, fist face upward, keep fists at the shoulder's level, at the same time, shift left fist to right elbow downward. Look straight ahead (Figure 2-7).

图 2-7(Figure 2-7)

5.单叉

(1)右腿向前弹踢,左腿弯曲;同时,上体右转,两臂前后向两侧摆掌。目视右前方(图 2-8)。

5.Single fork

(1) Right leg swings forward, left leg straight, at the same time, the upper

part of the turn right, arms into spearing palms .Look right forward (Figure 2-8).

图 2-8(Figure 2-8)

(2)上动不停,左脚蹬地跳起;同时,右脚落地,屈膝下蹲,左腿向左铲出成仆步,两臂由上向下经胸前向下按于体前,两掌指尖相对,掌心向下,肘微屈。目视左前方(图 2-9)。

(2) Keep moving, left foot falls and jumps, at the same time, right foot falls, bend the knee and squat, left leg swings leftward into the drop stance, shift arms from downward to the chest and press in front of the crotch, palm fingertips against each other, palm centers downward, elbow slightly bends. Look left forward (Figure 2-9).

图 2-9(Figure 2-9)

6.怀中抱月

(1)身体上起,向右微转,两腿由全蹲变为半马步;同时,两掌向下,向身体两侧撑掌。目视右下方(图 2-10)。

6.Holding moon in arms

(1) Arise, turn right a little, change two legs from all squat into semi-horse-riding; at the same time, palm centers downward, extend and swing on

both sides. Look at right downward (Figure 2-10).

图 2-10(Figure 2-10)

(2)上动不停,身体重心移至左腿,右脚向左一步同左脚并拢;同时,两臂屈肘摆掌,两掌心相对,右肘与肩同高。目视左前方(图2-11)。

(2) Keep moving, shift gravity center to left leg, right foot to left a step and close right foot to left foot, at the same time, bend the elbow and put the palm, palm centers against each other, make right elbow and shoulder at the same height. Look left forward (Figure 2-11).

图 2-11(Figure 2-11)

7.仆步切掌

(1)两腿屈膝微下蹲;同时,右掌向下左掌向上,两掌根相对在胸前相交。目视右掌(图 2-12)。

7.Bend and cut palm

(1)Bend the knees and squat a little; at the same time, right palm downward and left palm upward, cross palms against each other on the chest. Look at right palm (Figure 2-12).

图 2-12(Figure 2-12)

(2)上动不停,两掌以掌根为轴顺时旋腕变成左掌在上,右掌在下;同时,左腿向上提膝。目视左前下方(图 2-13)。

(2) Keep moving, as the palm root axis, make two palms rotate the wrist clockwise then change left palm upward, right palm downward; at the same time, lift the left knee. Look left forward downward (Figure 2-13).

图 2-13(Figure 2-13)

(3)左腿向前下方切掌,右腿屈膝下蹲成仆步;同时,右掌变拳收抱腰间,左掌向下方切掌。目视左掌(图 2-14)。

(3) Make left leg forward downward cut palm, bend right knee and squat; at the same time, change right palm into fist and close at the waist, make left palm downward cut palm. Look at left palm (Figure 2-14).

图 2-14(Figure 2-14)

8.弓步冲拳

(1)身体上起,两腿弯曲成半马步;同时,左掌向身体左侧搂手,右拳收抱腰间。目视左掌(图2-15)。

8.Keep legs still and punching

(1) Arise, bend legs into semi-horse-riding; at the same time, let left palm to the left side of the body and build a hand, close right fist at the waist. Look at the left palm (Figure 2-15).

图2-15(Figure 2-15)

(2)右腿蹬地,左腿屈膝前弓成左弓步;同时,左掌向左搂抱腰间,右臂随身体左转的力量向前冲拳,拳心向下。目视前方(图2-16)。

(2) Stamp the right leg to ground, bend left knee into left leg still; at the same time, move left palm left and hold the waist, follow the strength of turning body left, let left arm forward and punch, make fist center downward. Look at forward (Figure 2-16).

图2-16(Figure 2-16)

(3)重心移至左腿,右腿由屈到伸,向前踢摆;同时,左拳变掌向前击拍右脚面,右拳收抱腰间。目视前方(图2-17)。

(3) Shift gravity center to left leg, bend and stretch right leg, kick and swing forward, at the same time, change left fist into palm forward and pat right

instep, close right fist against the waist. Look straight ahead (Figure 2-17).

图 2-17(Figure 2-17)

（4）上动不停,左腿弯曲,右腿向后落步成左弓步;同时,左掌变拳收抱腰间,右拳向前冲出,拳心向下。目视前方(图 2-18)。

(4) Keep moving, bend left leg, right leg falls backward into the left bow stance, at the same time, change left palm into fist against waist, right fist forward, fist center downward. Look at punching target. Look straight ahead (Figure 2-18).

图 2-18(Figure 2-18)

9.转身背后捶

（1）左腿伸直,右腿弯曲,身体右后转180°,右臂屈肘随转体向右顶肘。目视顶肘方向(图 2-19)。

9.Turning punch

(1) Left leg straight, bend right leg, turn 180°rightward and backward, bend right elbow, turn and butt right elbow rightward. Look butting target (Figure 2-19).

图 2-19(Figure 2-19)

(2)上动不停,身体继续右转,右脚尖外展,左腿向右腿靠拢,两腿全蹲成歇步;同时,右拳收抱腰间,左拳向前冲出,拳心向下。目视左拳(图 2-20)。

(2) Keep moving, turn right, outreach right tiptoes, close left leg to right leg, legs with spring sitting into the sitting stance, at the same time, close right fist against the waist, punch left fist forward, fist center downward. Look at left fist (Figure 2-20).

(a)正(Front)　　(b)反(Back)

图 2-20(Figure 2-20)

第二段

Section 2

10.架起捶

(1)两腿上起,身体左转;同时,右拳变掌向前下方插击,拳心斜向上,左拳变掌,屈臂挟于右小臂上。目视插掌方向(图 2-21)。

10. Parrying fist

(1) Change leg spring sitting into squatting, turn left, at the same time, change right fist into palm and spear it forward and downward, palm center obliquely upward, change left fist into palm and thrust it on the right forearm. Look at spearing target (Figure 2-21).

第二章　少林罗汉拳

图 2-21（Figure 2-21）

（2）上动不停,左脚向前上一步屈膝下蹲,身体右转成弓步;同时,右掌变拳上架至右额角上方,拳心向外。左掌变拳向左前方冲出,拳心向下。目视左拳(图 2-22)。

（2）Keep moving, left foot strides a step forward, turn right, at the same time, change right palm into fist and parry it rightward to right forehead. Fist center outward, change left palm into fist and parry it to upward to right forehead, fist center downward. Look at the left fist (Figure 2-22).

图 2-22（Figure 2-22）

11.转身斜劈掌

上体左转成左弓步,左拳收抱腰间,右拳变掌随转体由右向下、向前劈掌,掌心斜向上。目视右掌(图 2-23)。

11.Turning and chopping palm

The upper part of turn left into the left bow stance, close left fist against the waist, change right fist into palm, turn and chop the palm downward and forward from rightward, palm center obliquely upward. Look at right palm (Figure 2-23).

53

图 2-23（Figure 2-23）

12.提鞋蹬腿

（1）重心稍前移,右臂屈肘摆至左胸前,掌心向下；同时,左拳变掌,直臂上摆,与肩同高,掌心向下。目视前方(图 2-24)。

12.Lifting and kicking

(1)Shift gravity center slightly forward, bend right arm, lower and swing elbow to the front of the chest, palm center downward, at the same time, change left fist into palm and swing it upward, keep it at the shoulder's level, palm center downward. Look straight ahead (Figure 2-24).

图 2-24（Figure 2-24）

（2）上动不停,重心向前移至左腿,左腿微屈；右脚由后摆至左腿前向上勾踢；同时,两掌向身体右斜下方摆击,掌心斜向下。目视右掌(图 2-25)。

(2) Keep moving, shift gravity center to left leg, bend left leg slightly. Swing right foot from backward to the front of left leg for kicking, at the same time, swing palms downward and rightward, palm center slantingly downward. Look at right palm(Figure 2-25).

第二章　少林罗汉拳

图 2-25（Figure 2-25）

（3）紧接上动,右腿屈膝上提,两掌变拳收抱腰间,拳心向上。目视前方(图 2-26)。

（3）Keep moving, bend and lift right knee, change palms into fists and close them rightward against waist, fist center upward. Look straight ahead (Figure 2-26).

图 2-26（Figure 2-26）

（4）上动不停,右腿由屈变伸,向右侧踹出,力达脚跟。两拳收抱腰间。目视右腿(图 2-27)。

（4）Keep moving, stretch right leg, kick rightward, keep it at the waist's level, close fists against the waist. Look at right leg (Figure 2-27).

图 2-27（Figure 2-27）

55

13.倒步连三掌

(1)左腿弯曲,右腿下落,身体左转成左弓步;同时,左拳变掌向左推出,右拳变掌抱于腰间。目视左掌(图2-28)。

13.Retreating and repeated chopping

(1) Bend left leg, right leg falls, turn left into the left bow stance, at the same time, change left fist into palm and push it leftward, change right fist into palm against the waist. Look at left palm(Figure 2-28).

图2-28(Figure 2-28)

(2)重心移向右腿,右腿蹬地向后跳起,左腿回收提膝,身体腾空;右掌向前推掌,左掌变拳抱于腰间。目视右掌(图2-29)。

(2) Shift gravity center to right leg, kick right leg backward jump, bend left knee, and jump. Push right palm forward, change left palm into fist against the waist. Look at right palm (Figure 2-29).

图2-29(Figure 2-29)

(3)上动不停,左右脚先后依次落地成左弓步;同时,右掌变拳收抱腰间,左拳变掌向前推出。目视左掌(图2-30)。

(3) Keep moving, left foot forward and right foot backward into the left bow stance, at the same time, change right palm to fist against waist, change left fist into palm and push it forward. Look at left palm(Figure 2-30).

图 2-30(Figure 2-30)

14.转身夯地捶

(1)右拳变掌由腰间向下摆击,左掌屈肘收于左肩前。目视右后方(图 2-31)。

14.Turning and ramming

(1) Change right fist into palm and swine it downward from waist, bend and swing left palm upward. Look right and backward (Figure 2-31).

图 2-31(Figure 2-31)

(2)上动不停,身体右转,成右弓步;同时,左掌由面前向身体右胸前摆掌,右掌内旋向里摆掌。目视左前下方(图 2-32)。

(2) Keep moving, turn right into the right bow stance, at the same time, press left palm to the front of the chest, swing right palm inward. Look left front downward (Figure 2-32).

图 2-32（Figure 2-32）

（3）紧接上动,左腿向前一步,同右脚并拢,两腿屈膝半蹲,左脚尖点地,重心在右腿,上体前倾;同时,两掌变拳,右拳由腹前经左臂内侧向前屈臂劈拳,左拳抱于腰间。目视右拳(图2-33)。

（3）Close left leg to right leg, bend knees on semi-crouch balance, left tiptoes touchdown, shift gravity center to the right leg. Lean forward, at the same time, change palms into fists, chop right fist via abdomen to left arm inward, left fist against the waist. Look at right fist (Figure 2-33).

图 2-33（Figure 2-33）

（4）上动不停,两腿屈膝下蹲,右脚前脚掌着地,左脚脚跟提起;右拳随上体前俯向下砸拳,拳心向内。目视右拳(图2-34)。

（4）Keep moving, make leg spring sitting, right sole touchdown, lift left heel, lean forward and smash right fist on the floor, palm center leftward. Look at right fist (Figure 2-34).

图 2-34（Figure 2-34）

第二章　少林罗汉拳

15.撑臂后蹬腿

身体上起,右腿屈膝支撑重心;同时,左腿由屈到伸向后蹬腿,脚尖勾起,力达脚跟。右臂撑直向下冲拳,拳面着地;左拳抱于腰间。目视左腿(图 2-35)。

15.Extending retreating and kicking

Right leg straight to support gravity center, at the same time, bend left leg for kicking backward, hook tiptoes hook upward, right straight for punching downward, fist face touchdown, close left fist against the waist. Look at left leg (Figure 2-35).

图 2-35

16.劈腿卧地捶

(1)左脚向前下落于右脚前方,身体上起直立;同时,右臂向上勾拳,拳心向里,拳面与肩同高。目视前方(图 2-36)。

16.Lying and chopping

(1) Left foot falls in front of right foot, stand upright, at the same time, right arm upward for punching, palm center inward, keep fist face at the shoulder's level. Look straight ahead (Figure 2-36).

图 2-36 (Figure 2-36)

59

（2）紧接上动，右腿由后向前上踢出，脚尖勾起，左腿伸直，支撑重心；同时，右拳由上向下劈拳。目视前方（图2-37）。

(2) Left leg straight, support the gravity center, right leg kicks out from backward, tiptoes hook upward, at the same time, right fist chops downward. Look straight ahead (Figure 2-37).

图2-37（Figure 2-37）

（3）上动不停，右腿自然下落，右脚在前，左脚在后成开立步，两拳收抱腰间。目视前方（图2-38）。

3) Keep moving, right leg naturally falls into the shoulder-width stance, withdraw fists to the waist. Look straight ahead (Figure 2-38).

图2-38（Figure 2-38）

（4）紧接上动，重心前移；左腿向前一步，两腿屈膝下蹲，右脚尖点地；同时，右拳向上，左拳向下，两拳心向后。目视左后方（图2-39）。

(4) Shift gravity center forward, left leg strides one step, bend knees and squat, right tiptoes touchdown, at the same time, right fist upward, left fist downward, and palm centers backward. Look at leftward and backward (Figure 2-39).

图 2-39(Figure 2-39)

(5)上动不停,两腿屈膝下蹲成坐盘;同时,左拳向下置于右脚脚腰上,拳心向后。右拳向上;拳面贴于太阳穴处,拳心向后。目视左上方(图 2-40)。

(5) Keep moving, bend knees and squat, at the same time, left fist downward to the right foot, fist center backward. Right fist face against the temple, fist center backward. Look leftward and upward (Figure 2-40).

图 2-40(Figure 2-40)

17.右转拉弓势

(1)向右转体 180°,两腿屈膝半蹲成马步;同时,右拳收至左肩前,拳心向里,左拳收抱腰间。目视右拳(图 2-41)。

17. Rightward turning and bow pulling

(1) Turn right 180°, bend knees on semi-crouch balance the horse-riding stance, at the same time, close fists to the front of the left shoulder, fist center inward, bend elbows. Look at right fist(Figure 2-41).

图 2-41(Figure 2-41)

(2)上动不停,右臂向后顶肘,小臂与肩同高,拳心向里,左拳向左侧冲出,拳心向外。目视左拳(图2-42)。

(2) Thrust right elbow backward, keep forearm at shoulder's level, palm center downward, punch left fist leftward, palm center downward. Look at left fist(Figure 2-42).

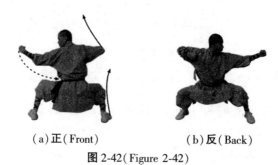

(a)正(Front)　　(b)反(Back)

图2-42(Figure 2-42)

18.转身底手炮

(1)重心移至左腿上,右腿提膝,身体随即右转90°;同时,右拳变掌向上架至头顶,掌心向下,左拳变掌,下落至胯前。目视前方(图2-43)。

18.Turning and punching

(1)Shift gravity center to left leg, lift right knee, turn rightward 90°, at the same time, change right fist into palm and parry it overhead, palm center downward, change left fist into palm and make it fall to the front hip. Look straight ahead (Figure 2-43).

图2-43(Figure 2-43)

(2)上动不停,以左脚为轴,继续向右转体90°;同时,右掌变拳向下落至胸前,拳心向上,左掌置于腹前,掌心向上。目视右拳(图2-44)。

(2) Keep moving, turn rightward 90°with left foot as the axis, at the same time, change right palm into fist and make it fall in the front of the chest, palm center upward, left palm against abdomen, supinely. Look at right fist(Figure 2-44).

图 2-44(Figure 2-44)

(3)上动不停,右脚向下落地并震脚,全脚掌着地,两腿并拢半蹲;同时,右拳向下砸拳,拳心向上置于左掌心内。目视右拳(图 2-45)。

(3) Keep moving, right foot falls and stamps, sole touchdown, legs close and partly squat, at the same time, and right fist falls and punches, fist back and left palm center against each other. Look at right fist (Figure 2- 45).

图 2-45(Figure 2- 45)

第三段

Section 3

19.坐山势

(1)左脚向左侧横跨一步屈膝下蹲成马步;同时,两拳向上由胸前向两侧左右劈拳,拳心向前。目视右拳(图 2-46)。

19.Mountain riding

(1) Left foot strides a step leftward into the horse-riding stance, at the same time, fists upward and separately, fist center forward. Look at right fist (Figure 2-46).

图 2-46(Figure 2-46)

(2)上动不停,两肘弯曲内收,两拳由上向下栽于膝上,拳心向斜后方。目视正前方(图 2-47)。

(2) Feet remain still, fists fall inward and against knees, fist center obliquely backward. Look straight ahead (Figure 2-47).

图 2-47(Figure 2-47)

20.抖毛

(1)双脚向身体左侧同时蹬地、跳起、腾空,两臂随身体自然摆动(图 2-48)。

20.Shaking hair

(1)Jump, arms swing naturally (Figure 2-48).

图 2-48(Figure 2-48)

第二章　少林罗汉拳

（2）紧接上动,左右脚先后依次落地,两腿下蹲成马步;同时,上体微左转,两臂带肩随转体前后摆动。目视右拳方向(图2-49)。

(2) Keep moving, foots fall into the horse-riding stance, at the same time, slightly turn left, and arms swing naturally. Look at right fist (Figure 2-49).

图 2-49(Figure 2-49)

（3）上动不停,上体向右转体,右臂向后,左臂向前自然摆动;同时,左腿随转体微扣膝、转髋。目视左拳方向(图2-50)。

(3) Keep moving, turn right, right arm backward, left arm forward, naturally swing, at the same time, left knee buckles slightly and hips turn. Look at left fist (Figure 2-50).

图 2-50(Figure 2-50)

（4）上动不停,身体向左转体,两腿下蹲成马步,两拳抱于腰间。目视前方(图2-51)。

(4) Keep moving, turn right, right arm backward, left arm forward, naturally swing, at the same time, left knee buckles slightly and hips turn. Look at left fist (Figure 2-51).

图 2-51(Figure 2-51)

21.左转上步一拳

身体左转180°;同时,右脚向左上一步成右弓步,右拳随右脚向前上步的同时向上勾拳,拳心向里,力达拳面。目视右拳(图2-52)。

21.Leftward turning and punching

Turn left 180°, at the same time, right foot strides a step into the right bow stance, and right fist strides a step forward with right foot, at the same time hook fist upward, fist center inward. Look at right fist (Figure 2-52)

图 2-52(Figure 2-52)

22.转身弹腿推掌

身体重心向前移至右腿,上体左后转;同时,左腿随转体向前弹出,右拳变掌向前推掌。目视前方(图2-53)。

22.Turning and kicking

Turn leftward and backward, at the same time, right leg straight to support gravity center, left leg kicks outward, change right fist into palm and make it push forward. Look straight ahead (Figure 2-53).

图 2-53(Figure 2-53)

第二章 少林罗汉拳

23.转身飞里拔腿

(1)左腿下落成提膝,上体右转90°;同时,左拳变掌上架至头顶上方,右掌变拳向身体后斜下方摆击,拳心向后。目视右拳(图2-54)。

23.Turning and kicking in the air

(1)Lift left knee, turn rightward 90°, at the same time, change left fist into palm and make it overhead, change right palm into fist and make it strike obliquely backward, fist center backward. Look at right fist (Figure 2-54).

图 2-54(Figure 2-54)

(2)紧接上动,左脚下落,右脚随即蹬地跳起向右后方屈膝后摆,上体微前倾,左掌架于头顶上方,右拳向下摆击。目视右下方(图2-55)。

(2)Keep moving. Left foot falls, and right foot jumps at once and swings right backward, upper body slightly bends forward, left palm overhead, right fist swings downward. Look at right downward (Figure 2-55).

图 2-55(Figure 2-55)

(3)上动不停,左腿屈膝半蹲,右脚擦地向左前方勾踢,脚尖外摆;同时,上体向右拧转,右掌变拳屈肘向右格挡,右掌扶于右肘窝处,掌心向下。

目视右拳方向(图2-56)。

(3) Keep moving, bend left knee and squat, right foot kicks leftward and forward, outreach tiptoes, at the same time, turn and twist rightward, change right palm into fist and make it parry rightward, close right palm to right cubital fossa, palm center downward. Look at right fist (Figure 2-56).

图 2-56(Figure 2-56)

24.撞金钟

(1)右脚向右前方上一步,左腿随即屈膝上提;同时,左掌变拳向下摆击,拳心向后,右拳回收至右肩前。目视左前方(图2-57)。

24.Bell bumping

(1) Right foot strides one step right forward, left knee at one bends and lift upward, at the same time, change left palm into fist and swings downward, fist center backward, right fist withdraws to the front of right shoulder. Look left forward (Figure 2-57).

图 2-57(Figure 2-57)

(2)腾空后,两拳抱于腰间,两腿自然弯曲(图2-58)。

(2) Withdraw fists to the waist in the air, and bend legs naturally (Figure 2-58).

图 2-58(Figure 2-58)

(3)上动不停,左腿、右腿依次落地成右弓步,低头、含胸,上体向左拧身(图 2-59)。

(3) Keep moving, legs fall into the bow stance, head down on chest, and turn slightly leftward (Figure 2-59).

图 2-59(Figure 2-59)

(4)紧接上动,上体向右甩腰,抬头挺胸。目视右方(图 2-60)。

(4) Turn and swing waist rightward, look up and throw out chest. Look right (Figure 2-60).

图 2-60(Figure 2-60)

25.转身双冲肘

(1)紧接上动,两拳收至胸前,两肘弯曲,左拳变掌,掌心置于右拳拳面。目视左后方(图2-61)。

25.Turning and double punching

(1)Close fists to the front chest, change left fist into palm, palm against the right fist face, and bend elbows. Look at left backward (Figure 2-61).

图2-61(Figure 2-61)

(2)上动不停,上体微右转,右肘随身体右转的同时向前顶肘,力达肘尖,肘尖与肩同高。目视右肘(图2-62)。

(2)Keep moving, turn right slightly, left palm pushes right palm to make it butt rightward, keep the arm at the shoulder's level. Look at right elbow (Figure 2-62).

图2-62(Figure 2-62)

(3)紧接上动,重心移至右腿,身体向右转体180°,左腿随身体右转时向上提膝;同时,右拳向下、向上曲臂收肘置于右胸前,拳心向下,左掌随右臂摆动置于胸前屈肘,掌心贴于右拳面上。目视左前方(图2-63)。

(3)Turn 180° rightward with right leg as the axis, left left knee, at the same time, bend right elbow and swing it rightward, swing left palm and right arm to the front of the chest, palm center against the right fist face. Look left forward (Figure 2-63).

图 2-63(Figure 2-63)

（4）上动不停，左腿向左前方下落步成弓步；同时，右拳变掌，左掌变拳，右掌按于左拳面上向前推左拳使左肘向前顶出，力达肘尖。目视左肘（图 2-64）。

(4) Keep moving, left leg falls leftward into the horse-riding stance, at the same time, change right fist into palm, change left palm into fist, right palm pushes left fist and make left elbow forward and butt. Look at left elbow (Figure 2-64).

图 2-64(Figure 2-64)

26.上步抢手

（1）右腿屈膝向前提膝；同时，左拳抱于腰间，右掌收至腰间，掌心向上。目视前方(图 2-65)。

26.Step advancing and palming

(1) Bend and lift right knee, left leg straight to support gravity center, at

71

the same time, close left fist to the waist, close right palm against the waist, supinely. Look straight ahead (Figure 2-65).

图 2-65(Figure 2-65)

(2)上动不停,右腿向前落步成右弓步;同时,右掌向前插掌,力达指尖,掌心向上,与鼻同高。目视右掌(图 2-66)。

(2)Keep moving, right leg falls forward into the bow stance, at the same time, right palm center forward and swings outward, supinely, keep it at the nose's level. Look at right palm (Figure 2-66).

图 2-66(Figure 2-66)

27.蹲桩捶

(1)右脚碾地,重心移至两腿中间,上体稍左转;同时,左臂屈肘上提至胸前,右掌变拳收至右肩前。目视左前方(图 2-67)。

27.Piling punch

(1)Right leg stretches slightly, shift gravity center to the crotch, turn leftward slightly, at the same time, lift left elbow to the front chest, change right palm into fist and make its lifted to the shoulder. Look left forward (Figure 2-67).

图 2-67（Figure 2-67）

（2）上动不停，上体继续左转，右脚向左前方上步同左腿并拢，两腿屈膝半蹲；同时，左臂屈肘回收与肩平行，拳心向下，右拳经耳旁向前冲出，拳心向下。目视右拳（图 2-68）。

（2）Keep moving, turn left, close left leg to right leg, bend knees on semi-crouch balance, at the same time, bend left elbow and keep it at the shoulder's level, fist center downward, right fist pushes forward by the ear, fist center downward. Look at right fist (Figure 2-68).

图 2-68（Figure 2-68）

第四段

Section 4

28. 卧枕势

（1）身体重心移至左腿，右腿屈膝向前提膝，右拳收抱于腰间，左拳由下向体前上方勾击。目视左拳（图 2-69）。

28.Sleeping and punching

(1) Left leg slightly stretches to support the gravity center, bend and lift right knee, close right fist against waist, swing left fist upward for striking. Look at left fist (Figure 2-69).

图 2-69(Figure 2-69)

(2)上动不停,右腿向前落步屈膝成弓步;同时,左臂曲肘回收,左拳向下,右拳由腰间向前移至腹前,拳心向上。目视左前下方(图 2-70)。

(2) Keep moving, right leg falls forward and slightly bends, shift gravity center to the right leg, at the same time, left fist falls against the abdomen, elbow tip upward, shift right fist in front of the abdomen, fist center inward. Look at left front downward (Figure 2-70).

图 2-70(Figure 2-70)

(3)上动不停,右腿屈膝,左腿伸直,右弓步不变,上体右倾斜;同时,右拳经腹前向上经左拳外侧屈臂上穿至右肩旁,拳心向后,右拳向下穿至左胯前,拳心向左,头向左摆。目视左后上方(图 2-71)。

(3) Keep moving, bend right knee on semi-crouch balance, left leg straight into the bow stance, lean obliquely rightward, at the same time, wave right fist

in front of the abdomen upward and bend left arm to right shoulder, fist center backward, right fist thrusts downward to the front of left hip, fist center leftward, turn left. Look at left backward (Figure 2-71).

图 2-71(Figure 2-71)

29. 老僧拔葱

(1)上体后仰,右腿伸直,重心移至左腿,两拳变掌,右掌向上摆击至右肩上方,左掌向上收于腹前,掌心向下。目视斜前下方(图2-72)。

29. Sudden jumping

(1) Lean back, right leg stretches slightly, shift gravity center to left leg, change fists into palms, shift right palm upward to above the shoulder, left palm in front of the abdomen, palm center downward. Look obliquely forward and downward (Figure 2-72).

图 2-72(Figure 2-72)

(2)上动不停,右腿屈膝半蹲,上体前俯,左腿蹬直成弓步;同时,右掌向斜前下方扑地,五指分开,掌心向下,左掌置于右肘处,掌心向下。目视右掌(图2-73)。

(2) Keep moving, bend right knee on semi-crouch balance, bend forward, left leg kicks straight, at the same time, right palm forward obliquely and pounces downward, fingers separate, palm center downward, close left palm at

the right elbow, palm center downward. Look at right palm (Figure 2-73).

图 2-73(Figure 2-73)

（3）紧接上动，右腿随身体后撤时，向后收半步，左腿屈膝下蹲，上体借右腿蹬地的同时向上立起。两掌变拳随上体立起向后上方外旋握拳。目视斜前下方（图 2-74）。

(3) Right leg straight, bend left leg slightly, right leg kicks and stand upright, at the same time, change right palm into fist and make it grab backward and upright. Look obliquely forward and downward (Figure 2-74).

图 2-74(Figure 2-74)

（4）上动不停，上体略向后倾斜，左腿支撑重心，右腿屈膝上提；同时，右臂屈肘向上提起至头右前方，左拳收至右膝上方，拳心向下。目视斜前下方（图 2-75）。

(4) Keep moving, slightly lean backward, left leg supports gravity center, bend and lift right knee, at the same time, and bend right elbow and lift it overhead. Look obliquely forward and downward (Figure 2-75).

图 2-75(Figure 2-75)

第二章 少林罗汉拳

30.蹲伸播种

紧接上动,右脚向前落步,左脚随即跟上,脚尖收于右脚腰处,两腿屈膝全蹲成丁字步,上体前俯;同时,右拳变掌向前向下按掌,掌心向下,左掌屈肘贴于右肩处。目视右掌(图2-76)。

30.Squatting and stretching

Right foot falls forward, left leg follows up, close legs and bend knees for spring sitting, bend forward, lift left heel, at the same time, change right fist into palm and make it swing forward and downward, palm center downward, bend left elbow against the right shoulder. Look at right palm (Figure 2-76).

图 2-76(Figure 2-76)

31.提鞋后蹬腿

(1)紧接上动,左脚向前上半步,右脚跟提起;同时,右掌收抱于腰间,左掌变拳向下冲拳。目视左拳(图2-77)。

31.Backward turning and kicking

(1)Bend knees on semi-crouch balance, left foot strides half a step forward and leftward, lift right heel, at the same time, close right palm against the waist, change left palm into fist and make it punch downward. Look at left fist (Figure 2-77).

图 2-77(Figure 2-77)

（2）紧接上动，右腿屈膝成跪步，右脚前掌着地，左腿屈膝半蹲；同时，左拳向内摆击，拳心向下，右掌向后抓握右脚跟部，掌心向后。目视右方（图2-78）。

（2）Right leg kneels, knee and front sole touchdown, bend left knee on semi-crouch balance, at the same time, left fist swings inward and strikes, palm center downward, right palm grasp right heel, palm center backward. Look at right backward (Figure 2-78).

图2-78（Figure 2-78）

（3）左腿上起，上体微右转前倾；同时，右腿由屈到伸向后蹬腿，脚尖勾起，力达脚跟，右臂向后伸直摆掌，左拳收于胸前。目视右脚（图2-79）。

（3）Left leg straight, turn slightly rightward and forward, at the same time, bend and stretch right leg and make it kick backward, hook tiptoes upward, right arm straight backward. Look at right foot (Figure 2-79).

图2-79（Figure 2-79）

32.二起脚

（1）右脚向前落步，重心前移，右掌变拳收于身体右后侧，左拳向前摆击于体前，拳心向下。目视前方（图2-80）。

32.Double kicking

(1)Right foot falls forward, shift gravity center forward, change right palm into fist, left fist stretches forward, fist center downward. Look straight ahead (Figure 2-80).

图 2-80(Figure 2-80)

(2)上动不停,身体重心移至右腿,屈膝下蹲,左腿向前上方摆踢;同时,左拳收至腰间,右拳变掌摆击至右肩前。目视前方(图2-81)。

(2) Keep moving, right foot falls, swing upward left leg, jump, at the same time, close left fist against the waist, change right fist into palm and shift it over the right shoulder. Look straight ahead (Figure 2-81).

图 2-81(Figure 2-81)

(3)上动不停,右脚蹬地,右腿向上方摆踢,身体腾空,左脚自然下落;同时,脚背绷直,右掌击拍右脚面,左拳收抱腰间。目视右脚(图2-82)。

(3) Keep moving, left foot naturally falls, at the same time, shift right leg upward, keep instep straight, right palm strikes right instep. Look at right foot

(Figure 2-82).

图 2-82(Figure 2-82)

33.束身双摆掌

（1）左脚落地,右脚随即向前落步,重心在两腿之间;同时,上体左转,左拳变掌,两掌分别向下、向左摆击,掌心向后。目视左掌(图2-83)。

33.Closing and double swinging

(1) Left foot falls, and right foot follows up, shift gravity center to the crotch, at the same time, turn left, palms downward, and swing leftward and backward. Look at left palm (Figure 2-83).

图 2-83(Figure 2-83)

（2）上动不停,左脚向前跟步成丁字步,左脚脚尖收于右脚脚腰处,两腿屈膝半蹲;同时,身体右转,两掌向上、向前摆掌,左掌收至右肩前,右掌心向外,左掌心向内。目视右掌(图2-84)。

(2) Keep moving, left foot follows up rightward, bend knees on semi-crouch balance, lift left heel, at the same time, turn right, palms upward, swing palms upward, rightward and forward, shift left palm to right elbow inward into raised palm. Look at right palm (Figure 2-84).

图 2-84(Figure 2-84)

34.里扫堂腿

(1)身体重心移至左腿,屈膝下蹲,右腿向前侧伸出成仆步;同时,两掌扶于地面。目视右下方(图 2-85)。

34.Sweeping and kicking

(1) Turn left, left foot stands firm, left leg spring sitting, right leg stretches rightward into the drop stance, at the same time, hold palms on the floor. Look at right downward (Figure 2-85).

图 2-85(Figure 2-85)

(2)紧接上动,右脚掌贴地,身体向右扭转,两手推地起身,右腿向前、向左扫腿。目视两掌(图 2-86)。

(2)Push hands and stand up, right leg sweeps forward below the hands. Look at the palms(Figure 2-86).

图 2-86(Figure 2-86)

（3）上动不停，两手自然下落，右腿继续左扫。目视下方（图2-87）。

（3）Keep moving, hands extend to the floor, right leg sweeps leftward. Look downward (Figure 2-87).

图2-87（Figure 2-87）

（4）上动不停，左腿屈膝上提；同时，右腿经左腿下方掏扫落地。目视下方（图2-88）。

（4）Keep moving, bend and lift left knee, at the same time, right leg sweeps rightward below the left leg. Look downward. (Figure 2-88).

图2-88（Figure 2-88）

（5）上动不停，两手扶于地面不动，左脚落地，右腿由后向右扫腿一周后成仆步。目视右脚（图2-89）。

（5）Keep moving, hold hands on the floor and keep still, left foot falls, right leg sweeps rightward into the drop stance. Look at right foot (Figure 2-89).

图2-89（Figure 2-89）

35.老僧照镜

(1)紧接上动,身体上起,右脚向左上一步,两掌自然向上带起向左右两侧撑掌,两掌心向后。目视右掌(图2-90)。

35.Mirroring

(1)Stretch left leg slightly, shift right foot leftward, stand up, palms upward, palm center backward. Look at right palm (Figure 2-90).

图2-90(Figure 2-90)

(2)上动不停,两腿屈膝下蹲,右脚外碾,左脚跟点起,左腿贴于右小腿后;同时,右掌向上屈肘外旋后撩,掌心向后,肘尖向下,左掌向下扶在右肘下方,掌心向下。目视右后方(图2-91)。

(2) Keep moving, bend knees on semi-crouch balance, left leg against right foreleg backward, right palm upward and bend elbow for arc kicking, palm center rightward and backward, elbow tip downward, hold left palm on the right forearm, palm center downward. Look rightward and backward (Figure 2-91).

图2-91(Figure 2-91)

36.伏身摸瓜

两腿交叉不变,上体前俯;同时,右掌向前转掌下按,掌心向下,左掌置于右臂下方,掌心向下。目视右掌(图 2-92)。

36. Bending and searching

Cross legs, bend forward, at the same time, right palm touches downward, palm center downward, left palm below right arm, palm center downward. Look at right palm (Figure 2-92).

图 2-92(Figure 2-92)

37. 迎面撒

(1)左腿向前上一步;同时,身体随左脚上步的同时右转,右掌向前抓,上起时握拳随身体向右后摆击,拳心向内,左臂屈肘,左掌心向下摆至胸前。目视右拳(图 2-93)。

37. Head-on sweeping

(1) Legs straight, left leg strides one step, at the same time, turn right, change right palm into fist and swing it rightward and backward, bend left elbow to the front chest, left palm center downward. Look at right fist (Figure 2-93).

图 2-93(Figure 2-93)

(2)上动不停,两腿屈膝半蹲成马步;同时,身体迅速向左抖身,右小臂迅速屈肘,右拳变掌迅速向左扬手,五指分开,掌心向左前方。目视左前方(图 2-94)。

(2) Keep moving, bend knees on semi-crouch balance into the horse-riding stance, at the same time, bend right elbow, change right fist into palm and swing it leftward, fingers separated, palm leftward. Look leftward (Figure 2-94).

图 2-94(Figure 2-94)

38. 老僧端锅

(1)重心移至左腿,上体左转 90°;同时,右腿屈膝向前提起,左掌向前搂掌于腰间抱拳,右掌变拳向上架于头顶,拳心向上。目视前方(图 2-95)。

38. Holding and fetching

(1) Shift gravity center to left leg, turn leftward 90°, at the same time, bend and lift right knee forward, arms separated, palm center outward. Look straight ahead (Figure 2-95).

图 2-95(Figure 2-95)

(2)上动不停,右脚向下落于左脚内侧,两腿屈膝下蹲;同时,右臂向下收于腰间后再由两侧向前、向上双抢掌,掌心向上。目视前方(图 2-96)。

(2) Keep moving, bend left knee, right leg falls in the left foot inward, bend knees on semi-crouch balance, at the same time, arms downward and forward and thrust palms on both sides, supinely. Look straight ahead

（Figure 2-96）.

图 2-96（Figure 2-96）

39.跳起弹踢

（1）两腿不动,两臂由前经体侧向后摆。目视前方（图 2-97）。

39.Jumping and kicking

（1）Keep legs still, swing arms backward. Look straight ahead (Figure 2-97).

图 2-97（Figure 2-97）

（2）紧接上动,右脚蹬地跳起,身体腾空,两臂自然上摆（图 2-98）。

（2）Right foot jumps, jump, arms swing naturally upward (Figure 2-98).

图 2-98（Figure 2-98）

(3)紧接上动,两掌左右分开变拳收抱腰间;同时,右脚面绷直向上弹踢,力达脚尖,左腿自然下垂。目视前方(图2-99)。

(3) Hands separated, at the same time, left leg naturally falls and make right keel kick upward, hook tiptoes hook upward. Look straight ahead (Figure 2-99).

图2-99(Figure 2-99)

40.双抢手

上动不停,左右腿向后依次下落成右弓步;同时,右掌经腰间向前抢手,左拳收抱腰间。目视右掌(图2-100)。

40.Double grabbing

Keep moving, legs fall backward into the bow stance, at the same time, arms fall and thrust palms in front of the waist, left fist against right forearm inward, supinely, right palm straight. Look at right palm (Figure 2-100).

图2-100(Figure 2-100)

41.转身罗汉眉

(1)两脚向左碾地,上体左转90°成马步;同时,右掌变剑,指内收于右胸前，左拳变剑，指向上收至左胸前，两掌心向下。目视前方（图2-101）。

41. Turning Arhat eyebrow

（1）Right leg straight, turn leftward 90°, at the same time, change fists into finger pointing gesture and bend elbow in front of the chest, keep at the shoulder's level. Look straight ahead (Figure 2-101).

图 2-101（Figure 2-101）

（2）上动不停，两脚向左碾地，身体继续左转180°，两腿屈膝下蹲成歇步，两剑指随体左转的同时向上至头两侧，摆击剑指于眉梢处，掌心向前。目视前方（图2-102）。

（2）Keep moving, turn leftward 180°, at the same time, bend knees and squat into the sitting stance, shift finger pointing gesture upward, keep the head's level, shift finger pointing gesture to brow tips. Look straight ahead (Figure 2-102).

图 2-102（Figure 2-102）

42. 双展翅

两腿不动，两剑指向左右两侧摆击，掌心向上。目视左手方向（图2-103）。

42. Turning swinging

Keep legs still, shift finger pointing gesture leftward and rightward, stretch palm upward. Look at left hand (Figure 2-103).

图 2-103(Figure 2-103)

43.双架棚

紧接上动,两腿伸直,身体上起;同时,两臂由两侧向上架至头上方,指尖相对,掌心向上。目视前方(图2-104)。

43.Double parrying

Legs straight, at the same time, parry arms upward until overhead at both sides, fingertips against each other, palms upward. Look straight ahead (Figure 2-104).

图 2-104(Figure 2-104)

44.五子登科

(1)身体右转;同时,两掌变拳向下收抱腰间,重心移至左腿。目视前方(图2-105)。

44.Jumping and soaring

(1)Turn right, at the same time, palms fall against the waist and hold into fists, shift gravity center to left leg. Look straight ahead (Figure 2-105).

图 2-105（Figure 2-105）

（2）紧接上动,右脚向前上方踢摆;同时,右拳变掌向前拍右脚面,左拳收抱腰间。目视前方(图 2-106)。

(2) Right foot kicks and swings forward, at the same time, change right fist into palm and pat right instep. Look straight ahead(Figure 2-106).

图 2-106（Figure 2-106）

（3）右脚落地,重心移向右脚,左脚跟提起;同时,右掌变拳收抱腰间。目视前方(图 2-107)。

(3) Right foot falls, shift gravity center to the right foot, lift left heel, at the same time, close left palm to the waist into holding fist. Look straight ahead (Figure 2-107).

图 2-107（Figure 2-107）

(4)紧接上动,左脚向前上方踢摆;同时,左拳变掌向前拍左脚面,右拳收抱腰间。目视前方(图2-108)。

(4) Left foot kicks forward and upward, at the same time, change left fist into palm and pat left instep forward. Look straight ahead (Figure 2-108).

图2-108(Figure 2-108)

(5)左脚落地,重心移向左脚,右脚跟提起;同时,左掌变拳收抱腰间。目视前方(图2-109)。

(5) Left foot falls, shift gravity center to the left foot, lift right heel, at the same time, close left palm to waist into holding fist. Look straight ahead (Figure 2-109).

图2-109(Figure 2-109)

(6)紧接上动,身体向左拧腰,右小腿向后屈膝上踢,脚掌心向上;同时,左拳变掌向后下方拍击右脚掌,右拳收抱腰间。目视右脚(图2-110)。

(6) Twist waist leftward, bend right foreleg and kick upward, at the same time, change left fist into palm and make it pat right sole backward and downward. Look at right foot (Figure 2-110).

图 2-110(Figure 2-110)

（7）右脚向前上步，重心移至右腿，屈膝半蹲，上体左转前俯，两臂自然向右上摆动。目视下方(图 2-111)。

(7) Right foot strides forward, shift gravity center to right leg, bend knees on semi-crouch balance, turn left and bend forward, arms swing naturally rightward. Look downward (Figure 2-111).

图 2-111(Figure 2-111)

（8）上动不停，左脚向后上方摆起，右脚蹬地跳起，身体随即腾空、左转180°，右脚由外向里摆踢；同时，左掌在面前方迎击右脚掌。（图 2-112)。

(8) Keep moving, swing and lift left foot backward, right foot jumps, jump and turn leftward 180°, left leg naturally falls and right leg inward, at the same time, left palm strikes right sole (Figure 2-112).

图 2-112(Figure 2-111)

(9)接上动,左脚先落地,右脚随后落地并提膝,左掌在体前摆击,右拳置于身体右后方。目视左掌(图 2-113)。

(9)Left foot falls, at the same time, right leg falls, lift knee, hands separated. Look at left palm (Figure 2-113).

图 2-113(Figure 2-113)

(10)右脚下落至左脚旁并向下用力震脚;同时,身体左转向右拧腰,左腿屈膝,小腿向后上摆踢,右拳变掌向下拍击左脚掌。目视右掌(图 2-114)。

(10)Right foot falls near left foot and stamps, at the same time, turn left, twist waist rightward, bend left knee, foreleg kicks backward and upward, right hand pats left sole. Look at right palm (Figure 2-114).

图 2-114(Figure 2-114)

45.坐山势

(1)上动不停,左脚向左侧下方落步,两腿屈膝下蹲成马步;同时,右掌向上摆至胸前,掌心向上,左拳变掌屈肘收于右臂上,掌心向下。目视左前方(图 2-115)。

45.Mountain riding

(1)Keep moving, left foot falls leftward, and bend knees into the horse-riding stance, at the same time, swing right palm to the front chest, palm center upward, bend left elbow against the right upper arm. Look left forward (Figure 2-115).

图 2-115(Figure 2-115)

(2)上动不停,两腿保持弓步不动,右拳向上、向左架于头右上方,拳心向上;左掌变拳向下栽于左膝上,左臂微屈外展,拳心向后;头随右拳上摆的同时迅速左摆。目视左前方发"威"声(图 2-116)。

(2)Keep moving, keep legs still, right fist upward, swing leftward, parry it rightward, forward and overhead, thrust left fist downward to left knee, slightly bend left arm and make it outreach, swing right fist and turn left. Look leftward and cry "Wei" (Figure 2-116).

图 2-116(Figure 2-116)

46.收势

(1)左脚向右收步,两脚并拢,身体直立;两拳收于腰间成抱拳势。目视前方(图 2-117)。

46.Closing

(1)Close left foot rightward, close feet, stand upright. Close fists against waist into holding fists. Look straight ahead (Figure 2-117).

图 2-117(Figure 2-117)

(2)两拳变掌,两臂伸直下垂于身体两侧,成立正姿势(图 2-118)。

(2)Change fists into palms, arms straight and hang at both sides, stand at attention (Figure 2-118).

图 2-118(Figure 2-118)

第三章 少林长拳
Chapter 3 Shaolin Long Boxing

第一节 套路动作名称
Quarter 1 Routine Name

第一段
Section 1

1. 预备势(Preparation)

2. 海底捞沙(Pick up sand from the sea bottom)

3. 迎面扳手(Head-on wrestling)

4. 撩阴截把捶(Crotch kicking and intercepting)

5. 弓步撑膀(Bow stance arm extending)

6. 马步合身(Horse-riding closing)

7. 提地擎天(Punching downward and upward)

8. 震脚挤手炮(Stamping and squeezing)

9. 弓步冲拳(Bow stance punching)

10. 二起飞脚(Double flying and kicking)

11. 弓步双括(Bow stance doubling drawing)

12. 束身抱拳(Closing and holding fists)

第二段

Section 2

13. 左橛楔捶（Left pegging and wedging）

14. 凤凰单展翅（Phoenix spreading single wing）

15. 左右摇山（Mountain shaking）

16. 扳手推腰（Wrenching and pushing）

17. 虎扑（Tiger pouncing）

18. 金鸡独立（Golden rooster standing on one leg）

19. 回头望月（Back leg kicking）

20. 束身抱拳（Closing and holding fists）

第三段

Section 3

21. 右橛楔捶（Right pegging and wedging）

22. 十字阔步（Crossing and striding）

23. 马步前后冲拳（Horse-riding front and back punching）

24. 盘肘（Elbow hooking）

25. 虚步亮掌（Empty stance palming）

26. 黑虎掏心（Attacking chest）

27. 左二起脚（Left double kicking）

28. 海底炮（Continuous punching）

29. 燕子取水（Fast punching）

30. 霸王观阵（Mighty punching）

31. 掏鬓捶（Temple punching）

32. 磨腰掏肋捶（Waist punching）

33. 虎扑（Tiger pouncing）

34. 双抱膝（Knees punching）

35. 蹬足冲拳（Kicking and punching）

36. 虚步撩掌（Empty stance palming）

37. 收势（Closing）

第二节 套路动作图解
Quarter 2　　Figures of Routine Movements

第一段

Section 1

1.预备势

(1)两脚并立,两臂自然下垂于身体两侧,挺胸收腹。目视前方(图3-1)。

1.Preparation

(1) Feet parallel, arms fall naturally, stand at attention. Look straight ahead (Figure 3-1).

图 3-1(Figure 3-1)

(2)两臂屈肘上提,两掌变拳抱于腰间;同时,左脚向左一步,与肩同宽。目视前方(图3-2)。

(2) Bend elbows upward, change palms into fists against the waist, at the same time, left foot strides one step leftward, the same wide as the shoulders. Look straight ahead (Figure 3-2).

第三章　少林长拳

图 3-2（Figure 3-2）

2.海底捞沙

左拳向上贴于左胸前,拳心向里;右拳变掌向下按于身体右侧,身体微向左转;两腿屈膝下蹲,右脚尖点地置于左脚腰内。目视右前下方(图 3-3)。

2.Pick up sand from the sea bottom

Left fist upward against the left chest, palm center inward, change right fist into palm against right side, turn left slightly, bend knees and squat, right tiptoes touchdown. Look at right front downward (Figure 3-3).

图 3-3（Figure 3-3）

3.迎面扳手("扳手"又名"崩掌")

身体向右转,右掌向前扳手击出。掌心向里,掌指向上。目视右掌。左拳向下收抱腰间,同时,右脚向右前方上一步,屈膝前弓,成弓步。目视右掌掌尖(图 3-4)。

3.Head-on wrestling ("wrestling" also called "rebounding palm")

Turn right, right palm punches forward. Palm center inward, fingers upward. Look at right palm. Left fist downward and against the waist, right wrestles and right foot strides one step forward and rightward. Change front bow stance

99

into right bow stance. Look at right palm tip (Figure 3-4).

图 3-4(Figure 3-4)

4.撩阴截把捶

(1)右掌变拳收抱腰间;左拳变掌,掌心向后、向左胯后下方摆击。目视前方(图 3-5)。

4.Crotch grabbing kicking and intercepting

(1)Change right palm into fist against waist, change left fist into palm, palm center backward, swing and strike left hip backward and downward. Look straight ahead (Figure 3-5).

图 3-5(Figure 3-5)

(2)上动不停,左掌中指、无名指、小指弯曲成撩阴掌;左脚向前一步,屈膝前弓成左弓步;同时,左掌由左胯后下方向身体前上方摆击,置于体前,掌指向上,掌心向里,掌指与鼻同高。目视左掌(图 3-6)。

(2)Keep moving, bend left middle finger, ring finger and little finger into crotch grabbing palm, left foot strides one step forward, bend into the left bow stance, left foot strides and left palm strikes forward and upward from left hip backward and downward, against body, supinely, keep fingers at the nose's level. Look at left palm (Figure 3-6).

图 3-6(Figure 3-6)

（3）上动不停,左掌向上、向下外旋变阴手成覆盖掌后握拳下拉至腹前;右拳从腰间由下向上屈肘绕身向下砸拳于身体右下方;同时,右腿上步,身体左转,两腿屈膝下蹲,右脚尖点地,置于左脚内侧。目视右拳(图 3-7)。

（3）Keep moving, swing left palm upward, downward and outward, change it into fist and make it downward, swing right fist one circle upward against the waist, bend elbow and hit rightward and downward, right leg steps forward, turn left, bend knees and squat, right tiptoes touchdown and against left ankle. Look at right fist (Figure 3-7).

图 3-7(Figure 3-7)

5.弓步撑膀

右脚向前一步,先屈膝下蹲成马步之后,两脚掌同时向右碾地转髋成右弓步;同时,左拳向后摆击置于左腿上方,拳心向后;右拳屈肘向右斜上方撞肘,力达肘尖,拳心向里括住头。目视后前方(图 3-8)。

5.Bow stance arm extending

Right foot strides one step forward, bend knees and squat into the horse-riding stance, at the same time, sole rightward into the right bow stance, left fist backward and swing it to left leg upward, palm center backward, bend elbow and bump it obliquely upward and rightward, keep right fist at the elbow's level, palm center inward. Look back forward (Figure 3-8).

图 3-8(Figure 3-8)

6.马步合身

两肘同时向腰间夹肘,两拳收抱腰间,拳心向上,两肘紧贴两肋;同时,两脚掌向左碾地,两腿屈膝下蹲成马步;含胸收腹。目视前方(图 3-9)。

6.Horse-riding closing

Change fists into elbows against the waist, fist centers upward, elbows against the both sides of the chest, at the same time, soles grind leftward, bend knees and squat into the horse-riding stance, draw the chest and tighten up the belly. Look straight ahead (Figure 3-9).

图 3-9(Figure 3-9)

7.提地擎天

(1)提地:两拳变掌,腿脚不动,臀部下蹲,两肩下沉,双掌向下按于两膝外下侧。目视前方(图3-10)。

7.Punching downward and upward

(1)Punching downward: Change fists into palms, keep legs and feet still, buttocks squat, shoulders sink, palms press knees outward and downward. Look straight ahead (Figure 3-10).

图 3-10(Figure 3-10)

(2)擎天:两掌内旋变成撩阴手,向上摆臂上冲时,再变成双拳,双臂微合,腰往后撑,双拳同时上冲;拳心向内。目视正前方(图3-11)。

(2)Punching upward: Change palms into crotch grabbing, keep at the waist's level, change them into fists, arms slightly close, waist extends backward, fists punch upward, palm centers inward. Look straight ahead (Figure 3-11).

图 3-11(Figure 3-11)

8.震脚挤手炮

(1)身体向左微转,右拳向下收抱于腰前大腿上方,左拳变掌向下按至右拳上方。目视左前下方(图3-12)。

8. Stamping and squeezing

(1)Turn left slightly, right fist falls close to the waist and above thigh.

Change left fist into palm and press left palm above right fist. Look at left downward (Figure 3-12).

图 3-12(Figure 3-12)

（2）上动不停,身体左转,左掌向身体左侧平搂掌,掌心向下;同时,右腿屈膝上提,右拳向上提起至胸前,拳心向下。目视前下方(图 3-13)。

(2) Keep moving, turn left, close left palm leftward, at the same time, bend right leg and lift it upward, right fist upward into downward smashing fist. Look forward and downward (Figure 3-13).

图 3-13(Figure 3-13)

（3）上动不停,右脚向下震脚两脚并拢成半蹲势;同时,右拳向下,左掌向上在体前迎击,右拳击在左掌心内。目视前下方(图 3-14)。

(3) Keep moving, right foot stamps, partly squat, at the same time, right fist downward, left palm upward and resists, right fist strikes inside the left palm. Look forward and downward (Figure 3-14).

图 3-14(Figure 3-14)

第三章 少林长拳

9.弓步冲拳

(1)右脚向右后方迈一步,两腿屈膝下蹲成马步;同时,左掌变拳收抱腰间;右拳变掌向身体左下方按掌,掌心向下。目视右前下方(图3-15)。

9.Bow stance punching

(1)Right foot strides one step rightward and backward, bend knees and squat into the horse-riding stance, at the same time, change left palm into fist and close it against the waist, change right fist into palm and press it downward and leftward, palm center downward. Look rightward, forward and downward (Figure 3-15).

图 3-15(Figure 3-15)

(2)上动不停,右掌向右搂手,变拳收抱腰间;左拳向右上方冲拳,拳眼向上;同时,身体右转,两脚掌向右碾地成右弓步。目视左拳(图3-16)。

(2)Keep moving, swing right palm one circle rightward and change it into fist against the waist, left fist punches rightward, eye of fist upward, at the same time, sole grinds rightward into the right bow stance. Look at left fist (Figure 3-16).

图 3-16(Figure 3-16)

10.二起飞脚

上体前倾上起,左脚蹬地向上,右脚疾起弹踢;身体随步向上腾空跃起;同时,右拳变掌拍击右脚面,左拳收抱腰间。目视右掌(图3-17)。

10.Double flying and kicking

Lean forward and straight, left foot step into ground and jumped up, right foot kicks upward, jump, at the same time, change right fist into palm and resist right instep, close left fist against waist. Look at right palm (Figure 3-17).

图 3-17(Figure 3-17)

11.弓步双括

上动不停,右脚向前下方落地,屈膝前弓成右弓步;右掌变拳收抱腰间后,再与左拳同时向右前上方由外向里双裹拳,上身微向前倾,击中点与肋齐;两拳面相对,拳眼向上,拳心向内。目视前方(图3-18)。

11.Bow stance double drawing

Keep moving, right foot falls forward and downward, bend elbow forward into the right bow stance, change right palm into fist against waist, fists hit forward, upward and rightward, lean forward slightly, keep target at the rib's level, palm centers against each other, eye of fist upward. Look straight ahead (Figure 3-18).

图 3-18(Figure 3-18)

12.束身抱拳

身体左转180°,左拳收回置于腹左侧;右拳从右膝外侧向下、向上、向前兜击于膝前上方,与腰同高;左右两拳相互缠绕一圈后,左拳在前,右拳在后,沉肘,两拳置于胸前。在两拳缠绕的同时,左脚置于右脚前,身体下蹲成虚步。目视左前方(图3-19)。

12.Closing and holding fists

Turn left 180°, close left fist leftward and against the abdomen, right fist hits downward, upward and forward above the knee from its outward, keep it at the waist's level, fists wrap around each other, left fist followed by right fist, bend elbows, and shift fists against the chest, at the same time, close left foot in front of right foot, squat into the empty stance. Look leftward (Figure 3-19).

图3-19(Figure 3-19)

第二段

Section 2

13.左橛楔捶

身体上起,左腿向前一步,屈膝前弓成左弓步;同时,左拳向前下方冲击,右拳向右后上方冲击,两拳心向下,两拳成一斜直线。目视左拳(图3-20)。

13.Left pegging and wedging

Arise, left leg strides one step forward, bend knee forward into the left bow stance, at the same time, left fist impacts forward and downward, right fist impacts rightward, backward and downward, palm centers downward, make fists an oblique straight line. Look at left fist (Figure 3-20).

图 3-20(Figure 3-20)

14.凤凰单展翅

两脚向右碾地,身体右转180°成右弓步;同时,两拳收抱腰间变掌,由腰间再向右前方推出。右掌在前,掌心向外,左掌在后,掌心向里。目视右掌(图3-21)。

14.Phoenix spreading single wing

Feet grind rightward, turn right 180° into the bow stance, at the same time, close fists against waist and change them into palms, push them rightward and forward. Right palm in the front, palm center outward, left palm in the back, palm center inward. Look at right palm (Figure 3-21).

图 3-21(Figure 3-21)

15.左右摇山

(1)由右弓步变马步,双屈肘,立掌,摇肩晃膀,向左右两侧摇动,摇法如双环形;掌的转动上不过眉、下不过膝,两掌先后交叉,上下转动,两手不能接触。眼随掌转(图 3-22 和图 3-23)。

15. Mountain shaking

(1) Change right bow stance into the horse-riding stance, bend elbows, raise palms, shake shoulders like double rings, turn palms below eyebrows and above knees, cross and turn palms up and down, hands separated. Look at the palms (Figures 3-22 and Figures 3-23).

图 3-22(Figures 3-22)　　图 3-23(Figures 3-23)

(2)上体动作相同,要求同上。右腿向左腿后插步(图 3-24)。

(2) Movements different but requirements the same as above. Change horse-riding into the cheat stance (Figure 3-24).

图 3-24 (Figure 3-24)

(3)上动不停,上体动作左右相同,下体两腿前后交换相互插步三次。(手、眼、身协调配合)(图 3-25~图 3-28)。

(3) Keep on moving, moving cheat stance 3 times. (Hands, eyes and body coordination) (Figures 3-25-Figures 3-28).

图 3-25（Figures 3-25） 图 3-26（Figures 3-26）

图 3-27（Figures 3-27） 图 3-28（Figures 3-28）

16.扳手推腰

偷步摇臂，右腿向左腿前上一步，屈膝前弓成右弓步；右掌向右前方摆击，掌心向里；左掌在右掌摆击的同时向右推掌，掌心向外前。目视右掌（图3-29）。

16.Wrenching and pushing

Cheat stance arm rocking and right leg strides one step forward and upward, bend knees into the front bow stance, right palm strikes rightward and forward, palm center inward, right palm wrestles, at the same time, left palm pushes rightward, palm center outward and forward. Look at right palm (Figure 3-29).

图 3-29（Figure 3-29）

17.虎扑

(1)右脚向后撤一步,脚尖点地。身体重心移至左腿,屈膝下蹲成虚步;同时,右掌由下回收向上、向下在胸前划弧一周置于右膝前,掌指向前下方,掌心向内,左掌向后收置于左膝外侧,掌心向下。目视右掌(图3-30)。

17. Tiger pouncing

(1) Right foot strides one step backward, tiptoes touchdown. Shift gravity center to left leg, bend knees and squat into the empty stance, at the same time, right palm upward, left palm downward, turn a circle in front of the chest, right palm in front of right knee, left palm behind left knee inward. Look at right palm (Figure 3-30).

图 3-30(Figure 3-30)

(2)上动不停,右脚向前一步,屈膝前弓成右弓步;同时,身体微向前扑,左脚在随右脚向前迈进的同时,向前急摧步并向右脚靠近成右弓步。双掌同时向右前上方推出,掌心向前,与腰同高。目视两掌(图3-31)。

(2) Right foot strides one step forward, bend knees into the front bow stance. Lean forward slightly, left foot follows right foot, kicks and approaches right foot. Palms push rightward, forward and upward, keep it at the waist's level. Look at palms (Figure 3-31).

图 3-31(Figure 3-31)

18.金鸡独立

身体重心移至右腿,右脚向右蹬地,左腿向前提膝,身体微向右转;同时,两掌变拳,左拳向下置于左膝上,拳心向外;右拳向下、向后、向上摆击架于头顶上方,拳心向上。目视左前方(图3-32)。

18.Golden rooster standing on one leg

Shift gravity center to right leg, lift leg knee forward, turn rightward slightly, at the same time, change palms into fists, left fist downward against left knee, fist center outward, right fist hits downward, backward and upward and overhead, fist center upward. Look leftward (Figure 3-32).

图 3-32(Figure 3-32)

19.回头望月

左腿向下,落脚屈膝成左弓步;同时,左拳向上、右拳向下,两拳在胸前交叉后向体侧摆击,左拳呈反拳向左上方冲击,拳心向里;右拳呈反拳向右下方冲击,拳心向后,身体向左前倾,两臂在一条斜直线上。目视右后前方(图3-33)。

19.Back leg kicking

Left leg falls and bend knee into the left bow stance, at the same time, left fist upward, right fist downward, fists cross in the front of the chest, left fist reverses and impacts rightward and downward, palm center inward, palm center upward, lean leftward and forward, arms in an obliquely straight line. Look right back forward (Figure 3-33).

第三章　少林长拳

图 3-33（Figure 3-33）

20.束身抱拳

两脚向右碾地，屈膝前弓成右弓步；同时，左拳由左膝外侧向下、向前，经右膝前向上；右拳拳心向上屈肘，在胸前同左拳相互缠绕一周后，屈肘收置于胸前，右拳在前，左拳在后，两拳心向里。在两拳缠绕的同时，右脚向后收置于左脚前，脚尖点地屈膝下蹲成右虚步。目视右前方（图3-34）。

20.Closing and holding fists

Feet grind rightward into the right bow stance, at the same time, left fist pushes downward and forward via left knee outside, right fist center upward and bend elbow, fists cross a circle in front of the chest, bend elbow in front of the chest, right fist in the front, left fist behind, fist centers inward. Fists wind a circle, at the same time, close right foot backward to the left foot, tiptoes touchdown into the right empty stance. Look rightward and forward (Figure 3-34).

图 3-34（Figure 3-34）

第三段

Section 3

21.右橛楔捶

右脚向前上一步,屈膝前弓成右弓步,上身向右前下方微倾,右拳向右前下方冲击,拳心向下;左拳向左后上方冲击,拳心向内,拳眼向上成立拳;两拳成一斜直线。目视右前下方(图3-35)。

21. Right pegging and wedging

Right foot strides one step forward, bend knee into the front bow stance, turn right, turn rightward, forward and downward, right fist strikes rightward and downward, fist center downward, left fist impacts leftward, backward and upward, eye of fist upward, fist in an obliquely straight line. Look rightward, forward and downward (Figure 3-35).

图 3-35(Figure 3-35)

22.十字阔步

两拳屈肘收置于胸前,拳心向下;左脚向左侧斜前45°划弧趟步;右腿随左脚落地时向上提膝,身体重心在左腿。目视前方(图3-36)。

22. Crossing and striding

Bend and close elbows to the front of the chest, fist center inward, left foot swings leftward 45° obliquely, lift and advance right knee. Look straight ahead (Figure 3-36).

第三章 少林长拳

图 3-36（Figure 3-36）

23.马步前后冲拳

上动不停,右脚向身体右侧落步屈膝下蹲成马步;同时,身体微向下含胸再迅速向上抖身,两拳由胸前向前、后冲击;左拳向前,右拳向后。目视前方(图 3-37)。

23.Horse-riding front and back punching

Keep moving, right foot falls rightward into the horse-riding stance, at the same time, left fist swings downward and palm center downward, change right fist into edged fist, fist center leftward, left fist forward, right fist backward, fists hit. Look straight ahead (Figure 3-37).

图 3-37（Figure 3-37）

24.盘肘

右拳向前下方,左拳向后下方,同时收抱腰间后,两拳再向胸前上方盘环缠绕,先冲右拳,再冲左拳,连续向前冲击三次。目视前方(图 3-38)。

24.Elbow hooking

Right fist forward, close left fist against the waist, fists downward. Right

115

fist in front, left fist behind, wind to the front of the chest and make them impact forward 3 times. Look straight ahead (Figure 3-38).

图 3-38(Figure 3-38)

25.虚步亮掌

右脚向后退半步,左脚随即向后撤一步,身体重心移至右腿,左脚尖点地成左虚步;左拳变掌由右臂上方向前推击,掌心向前,指尖向上,右拳从左掌下方收抱腰间。目视左掌(图 3-39)。

25.Empty stance palming

Right foot retreats half a step, left foot follows, shift gravity center to right leg, left tiptoes touchdown into the left empty stance, change left fist into palm and make it butt forward, palm center forward, fingertips upward, close right fist against the waist. Look at left palm (Figure 3-39).

图 3-39(Figure 3-39)

26.黑虎掏心

左脚向前一步屈膝成左弓步,左掌向左搂手变拳收抱腰间。右拳向前冲拳,在右拳冲击的同时,右脚向前进半步成弓步。目视右拳(图 3-40)。

26.Attacking chest

Left foot strides one step forward and bend knee into the left bow stance, left palm brushes leftward and change it into fist and close it against the waist. Right fist impacts forward, at the same time, right foot advances half a step into the bow stance. Look at right fist (Figure 3-40).

图 3-40(Figure 3-40)

27.左二起脚

上动不停,上身微向前倾领劲,左脚用力向上蹬地向前弹踢,身体随步跃起;同时,左拳变掌向前拍击左脚面,右拳收抱腰间。目视前方(图3-41)。

27.Left double kicking

Keep moving, lean forward slightly, left foot kicks forward and upward, jump, at the same time, change left fist into palm and make it pat left instep, close right fist against waist. Look straight ahead (Figure 3-41).

图 3-41(Figure 3-41)

28.海底炮

紧接上动,身体右转 90°,两脚先后落地同时向下震脚;两脚并拢屈膝下蹲,两拳收抱腰间后再向下连续冲击三拳,先冲右拳,再冲左拳,在右拳冲至第三拳时左拳收抱腰间,右拳面向下,拳心向里。目视右前下方(图3-42)。

28. Continuous punching

Turn rightward 90°, feet fall and stamp, bend knees and squat into the chair piling stance, impact downward and rightward twice and leftward once continuously. Look right ahead downward (Figure 3-42).

图 3-42(Figure 3-42)

29. 燕子取水

(1)右拳收抱腰间,左拳变掌从身体左后侧向前下方撩掌摆击;同时,右脚向右一步,屈膝下蹲,身体微向右前方倾移。目视左掌(图3-43)。

29. Fast punching

(1) Close right fist against waist, change left fist into palm and swing it forward and downward from leftward and backward, at the same time, right foot strides one step rightward, bend knees and squat, lean rightward and forward slightly. Look at left palm (Figure 3-43).

图 3-43(Figure 3-43)

(2)左脚向前一步成左弓步;同时,左掌由下向上变撩阴掌,摆击于体前,掌心向上。目视左掌(图3-44)。

(2) Left foot strides one step forward into the left bow stance, at the same time, left palm upward, supinely. Look at left palm (Figure 3-44).

图 3-44(Figure 3-44)

(3)上动不停,身体左转,左掌外旋,向上、向左摆击,掌心向上。右拳变掌,与左掌同时从身体右侧向上、向下摆击于左胸前,掌心向下;同时,右腿向前上方提膝,左脚蹬地向前垫步跳起。目视左掌(图3-45)。

(3) Keep moving, turn left, left palm swings and strikes outward, upward and leftward, supinely, change right fist into palm, palms swing and strike upward and downward to left chest from rightward, palm centers downward, at the same time, bend and lift right knee, left foot stamps and jump. Look at left palm (Figure 3-45).

图 3-45 (Figure 3-45)

(4)上动不停,右腿屈膝下蹲成仆步;同时,两掌下按置于体前。目视左前上方(图3-46)。

(4) Keep moving, bend right knee and squat, swing left leg downward and leftward into the drop stance, at the same time, press palms downward. Look

leftward and upward (Figure 3-46).

图 3-46(Figure 3-46)

30.霸王观阵

身体上起,左腿向右前方收脚,身体重心移至右腿,左脚尖点地。左掌内旋成撩阴掌向左上方屈肘收置于右臂前,右掌变拳向头顶上方冲击,拳心向左前方。目视左前方(图 3-47)。

30.Mighty punching

Close left leg rightward and forward, shift gravity center to right leg, left tiptoes touchdown. change left hand into crotch grabbing palm, palm leftward and upward, bend elbow in front of right arm, change right palm into fist and make it impact upward, palm center leftward, rightward and overhead. Look leftward (Figure 3-47).

图 3-47(Figure 3-47)

31.掏鬓捶

(1)两腿屈膝下蹲成丁字步;同时,右臂向下屈肘,左掌随体下收在右肩前。目视左前方(图 3-48)。

第三章 少林长拳

31.Temple punching

(1) Bend knees and squat into the T-step, at the same time bend right elbow, left palm remains in front of right shoulder. Look leftward (Figure 3-48).

图 3-48 (Figure 3-48)

(2)左脚向前一步屈膝前弓,左掌向前推击,右拳向前冲击置于左掌上方,拳心向里。目视左前方(图 3-49)。

(2) Left foot strides one step forward into the front bow stance, right fist impacts forward, left palm putts forward, palm center forward and below the right fist. Look leftward (Figure 3-49).

图 3-49 (Figure 3-49)

32.磨腰掏肋捶

(1)左脚收回,身体下蹲成丁字步,左掌收置于右腰间,肘和掌贴紧腹部,掌心向右后方;同时,右拳向身体右后侧摆击,拳心向后。目视左前方(图 3-50)。

32. Waist punching

(1) Close left foot into the T-step, squat, close left palm against right

waist, palm center rightward and backward, close elbow and palm against abdomen, at the same time, right fist swings and strikes rightward and backward, fist center backward. Look leftward (Figure 3-50).

图 3-50 (Figure 3-50)

(2) 紧接上动,左脚向左前一步,身体左转180°,右脚随即向前一步,屈膝下蹲成马步;同时,左掌变楞拳由胸前向左侧身后抖肘横击,拳眼向上,拳心向前,右拳随身体左转时屈肘向胸前横击,拳心向后,拳眼向上,两拳心相对。身随拳拧转,拳与胸同高。目视右拳(图3-51)。

(2) Left foot strides one step forward and leftward, turn leftward 180°, right foot strides one step forward, bend knees and squat into the horse-riding stance, at the same time, change left palm into edged fist and make it strike leftward from the chest, right fist eye upward, bend elbow and make it swing to the front chest from rightward. Turn with fists, and keep fists at the chest's level. Look at right fist (Figure 3-51).

图 3-51 (Figure 3-51)

33.虎扑

(1) 两拳变掌收于腰间,再由胸前随身体右转的同时向下交叉旋转缠绕一周,右脚收置左脚前屈膝下蹲,右掌在前置于右膝外侧,左掌在后置于左膝外侧。目视右掌(图 3-52)。

33.Tiger pouncing

(1) Change fists into palms, cross and turn them a circle in front of the chest, close right foot against left foot, bend knee and squat, right palm in the front and right knee outward, left palm behind and left knee outward. Look at right palm (Figure 3-52).

图 3-52(Figure 3-52)

(2)右脚向前一步,身体微向前扑,左脚随即向前撺步跟进成弓步;同时,双掌向右前上方摆掌,右掌在前,左掌在后,两掌心相对。目视右掌(图 3-53)。

(2) Right foot strides one step forward, bend knee and strides half a step, lean forward slightly, left foot forward and approaches right heel, palms push rightward, forward and upward, palm centers against each other. Look at right palm (Figure 3-53).

图 3-53 (Figure 3-53)

34.双抱膝

身体右转 90°,重心移至右腿,左腿向前提膝;同时,双掌变拳,拳面向上,拳心向里,双肘紧靠在左膝两侧,含胸拔背。目视左前上方(图 3-54)。

34. Knees punching

Turn rightward 90°, lift leg knee forward, change palms into fists, fist faces upward, close elbows against both sides of left knee, draw the chest and extend the back. Look leftward, forward and upward (Figure 3-54).

图 3-54(Figure 3-54)

35. 蹬足冲拳

(1)上动不停,身体向右侧微倾,右脚向右踞地,左脚向左前方蹬击,力达脚跟;同时,右拳向右前斜下方冲击,左拳向左后上方冲击,与右拳成一斜平行线,两拳心向下。目视前方(图 3-55)。

35. Kicking and punching

(1) Keep moving, lean rightward slightly, left foot kicks leftward and forward, at the same time, right fist impacts rightward, forward and downward, left fist impacts leftward, backward and upward, fists in an oblique parallel line. Look forward (Figure 3-55).

图 3-55(Figure 3-55)

(2)两拳同时向腰间收拢,左脚自然向前下落,身体重心置于左脚,右脚随即提起。目视右前下方(图 3-56)。

(2) Close fists against the waist, left foot naturally falls, shift gravity center to left foot, right foot similar to an empty stance. Look rightward, forward and downward (Figure 3-56).

图 3-56(Figure 3-56)

(3)上动不停,左脚紧跟,向上垫步,右脚向前落步,屈膝前弓;两拳从腰间由外向内、向右前方弧形双裹拳,拳面相对,拳心向里。目视两拳(图 3-57)。

(3) Keep moving, lift right foot forward, left foot follows and makes a skip step, right foot falls forward, bend knee into the front bow stance, fists impact rightward and forward from hips, fist centers against each other, fist center upward. Look at fists (Figure 3-57).

图 3-57(Figure 3-57)

36.虚步撩掌

两脚掌向左碾地,身体左转 180°,左腿向右收脚,右腿屈膝下蹲,左脚尖点地;同时,右拳变掌从右膝外侧向体上撂掌,左拳变掌向上摆掌,两掌在胸前缠绕一周后,屈肘收置于胸前。左掌在前,右掌在后,两掌心向上。目视左前方(图 3-58)。

36. Empty stance palming

Soles grind leftward, turn leftward 180°, close left foot rightward, bend right knee and squat, left tiptoes touchdown, at the same time, change right fist into palm and make it swing right knee outward, change left fist into palm upward, wind palms a circle in front of the chest, bend elbow into tiger claw palm against the chest. Left palm in the front, right palm behind, palm centers upward. Look leftward (Figure 3-58).

图 3-58(Figure 3-58)

37.收势

(1)身体上起,两腿伸起,左腿向后收半步,身体右转,两掌变拳收抱腰间。目视前方(图 3-59)。

37. Closing

(1) Legs stretch, stand upright, palms against the waist into the holding fists posture. Look straight ahead(Figure 3-59).

图 3-59(Figure 3-59)

(2)两拳变掌,两臂伸直下垂于身体两侧,左脚向右脚靠拢,成立正姿势。目视前方(图 3-60)。

(2)Change fists into palms, arms straight and fall naturally, stand at attention. Look straight ahead (Figure 3-60).

图 3-60(Figure 3-60)

第四章 少林七星拳
Chapter 4 Shaolin Seven-star Boxing

第一节 套路动作名称
Quarter 1 Routine Name

第一段
Section 1

1. 预备势(Preparation)
2. 缩身钳子手(Shrinking pliers)
3. 十字弹踢(Cross kicking)
4. 缩身钳子手(Shrinking pliers)
5. 护耳掌(Ear protecting palm)
6. 单拍脚(Single foot tapping)
7. 弓步冲拳(Bow stance punching)
8. 下阴捶(Crotch fist)
9. 拐肘恨鞋(Cranking and kicking)
10. 三崩手(Crouching and palming)
11. 十字弹踢(Cross kicking)
12. 缩身钳子手(Shrinking pliers)

第二段
Section 2

13. 单拍脚(Single foot tapping)

14.左鸡型步(Left constant palming)

15.右鸡型步(Right constant palming)

16.左鸡型步(Left constant palming)

17.饿虎势(Vigorous palming)

18.小缩身(Shrinking fist)

19.十字弹踢(Cross kicking)

20.缩身钳子手(Shrinking pliers)

21.上步一捶(Striking fist)

22.又一捶(One more)

23.再一捶(Two more)

24.缩身钳子手(Shrinking pliers)

第三段

Section 3

25.十字弹踢(Cross kicking)

26.缩身钳子手(Shrinking pliers)

27.护耳掌(Ear protecting palm)

28.拐肘恨鞋(Cranking and kicking)

29.外摆莲(Outward palming)

30.斜一捶(Oblique punching)

31.下阴捶(Crotch fist)

32.拐肘恨鞋(Cranking and kicking)

33.三崩手(Crouching and palming)

34.十字弹踢(Cross kicking)

35.缩身钳子手(Shrinking pliers)

第四段

Section 4

36.二起脚(Double kicking)

37.双按掌(Double palming)

38.双撑肘(Double elbowing)

39.十字通背(Cross punching)

40.小缩身(Shrinking fist)

41.上步一捶(Striking fist)

42.又一捶(One more)

43.转身十字手(Turning and crossing)

44.收势(Closing)

第二节 套路动作图解
Quarter 2 Figures of Routine Movements

第一段

Section 1

1.预备势

(1)两脚并立,两臂自然下垂于身体两侧,挺胸收腹,成立正姿势。目视前方(图4-1)。

1.Preparation

(1)Feet parallel, arms fall naturally, throw out chest and withdraw abdomen, stand at attention. Look straight ahead (Figure 4-1).

图4-1(Figure 4-1)

(2)两臂屈肘向上提,两掌变拳抱于腰间;同时,左脚向左一步,与肩同宽。目视前方(图4-2)。

(2)Bend and lift elbows, change palms into fists against the waist, at the same time, left foot strides a step leftward, the same wide as shoulders. Look straight ahead (Figure 4-2).

图 4-2(Figure 4-2)

2.缩身钳子手

身体左转90°,右脚向左碾脚,脚尖扣在左脚脚腰内,两腿屈膝下蹲(大腿稍高于膝关节,敛臀挺胸,本套路此动作重复较多,凡出现此动作要求一样),左脚在前,右脚在后;同时,右拳变掌上提至胸前向体下插掌,置于右腿前,掌心向身体右外侧,掌指向下;左拳向右肩上方变掌上插于肩前,掌心向身体右外侧,掌指向上。目视左上方(图4-3)。

2.Shrinking pliers

Turn leftward 90 °, right foot grinds leftward, tiptoes buckle in the left instep, squat (legs slightly above the knees, close buttocks, throw out chest, repeat this movement quite a few times, with the same requirements), left foot in front, right foot behind, at the same time, change right fist into palm and swing it to the front of the chest and downward, and in front of the right leg, palm center rightward and outward, fingers apart and downward, swing left fist to right shoulder and change it into palm, palm center rightward and outward, fingers apart, fingers upward. Look leftward and upward (Figure 4-3).

图 4-3(Figure 4-3)

3.十字弹踢

(1)身体微向上起;同时,左掌向下置于右肘上方,掌心向下;右掌向上在胸前向下顺时针旋转手腕置体前,掌心向上。目视左前方(图4-4)。

3.Cross kicking

(1) Slightly rise, at the same time, swing left palm downward to above right elbow, palm center downward, swing right palm upward to the front of the chest and rightward. Look leftward and forward (Figure 4-4).

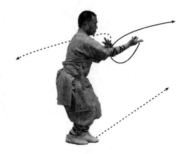

图4-4(Figure 4-4)

(2)上动不停,左腿向前弹击,脚面绷直,力达脚尖;同时,右掌向下收至胸前,由胸前再展臂向前弹击,力达指尖,掌心向里;左掌随右掌向前弹击的同时向后展臂弹击,掌心向上,力达掌指。目视右掌(图4-5)。

(2) Keep moving, close right palm downward and to the front of the chest, and swing arms forward, exert strength to fingertips, palm center backward, make left palm draw curve to the front of right palm and make it swing backward, palm center upward, fingertips backward, at the same time, swing left foot forward, instep straight, exert to tiptoes. Look at right palm (Figure 4-5).

图4-5(Figure 4-5)

第四章 少林七星拳

4.缩身钳子手

左脚向下收落至右脚前,两腿屈膝下蹲;同时,左掌经左肩上方向下压掌、收于左腿前侧,掌心向左外侧,指尖向下,右掌向下,经腹前向上内旋、收于左肩前,掌心向左外侧,指尖向上。目视左前方(图4-6)。

4.Shrinking pliers

Close left foot downward to the front of the right foot, squat, swing left palm upward and overhead, and to the front of the left leg, fingers apart, fingertips downward, swing right palm upward and in front of the abdomen and to the front of left shoulder, palm center leftward and outward, fingers apart, fingertips upward. Look leftward and forward (Figure 4-6).

图 4-6(Figure 4-6)

5.护耳掌

身体向右转90°,左腿向前一步,屈膝前弓;同时,右掌变拳收抱腰间,左掌从体侧向身体左上方摆击,置于左肩前,掌心斜向上。目视正前方(图4-7)。

5.Ear protecting palm

Turn rightward 90 °, left leg strides a step forward, bend knee into the front bow stance, at the same time, change right palm into fist against the waist, swing left palm leftward and upward from the right side, and to the front of left shoulder, palm center obliquely upward. Look straight ahead (Figure 4-7).

图 4-7(Figure 4-7)

6.单拍脚

右脚向上弹击,脚面绷直;同时,右拳变掌向前抢手拍击右脚脚面,左掌向下变拳收抱腰间。目视右掌(图 4-8)。

6.Single foot tapping

Right foot kicks upward, keep instep straight, at the same time, change right fist into palm and swing it forward to tap right instep, change left palm into fist against the waist. Look at right palm (Figure 4-8).

图 4-8(Figure 4-8)

7.弓步冲拳

右腿向下落脚,屈膝前弓;同时,右掌变拳收抱腰间,左拳由腰间向前冲出,拳心向下,与肩同高。目视前方(图 4-9)。

7.Bow stance punching

Right leg falls, bend knee into the front bow stance, at the same time, change right palm into fist and close it against the waist, swing left fist forward against the waist, fist center downward, at the shoulder's level. Look straight ahead (Figure 4-9).

图 4-9(Figure 4-9)

8.下阴捶

(1)两脚碾地,身体左转,两腿屈膝下蹲;左拳变掌收拉屈肘置于左肩上方,掌心向上,指尖向后;右拳抱至腰间。目视右前下方(图 4-10)。

8.Crotch fist

(1)Turn left, feet grind leftward, squat, change left fist into palm and bend elbow above left shoulder, palm center upward, fingertips backward, close right fist againstthe waist. Look rightward, forward and downward (Figure 4-10).

图 4-10(Figure 4-10)

(2)上动不停,右拳由腰间外旋向右腿后侧下冲拳,拳心向后。目视右拳(图 4-11)。

(2) Keep moving, swing right fist outward and right leg backward from the waist, palm center backward. Look at right fist (Figure 4-11).

图 4-11（Figure 4-11）

9.拐肘恨鞋

身体向左转 90°，右脚向前下震于左脚并拢，两腿屈膝下蹲（大腿与膝关节呈水平）；同时，右臂屈肘向左侧横击肘，左掌向下迎击在右肘臂上。目视左掌(图 4-12)。

9.Cranking and kicking

Turn leftward 90°, right foot stamps outside left foot and close them, squat, keep thighs and knees horizontal, at the same time, bend right elbow and make it swing leftward, left palm downward to pat right elbow. Look at left palm (Figure 4-12).

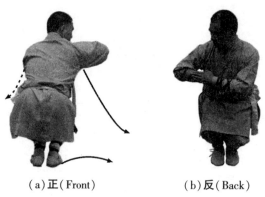

(a)正(Front)　　　(b)反(Back)

图 4-12（Figure 4-12）

10.三崩手

(1)右脚向右一步，两腿屈膝下蹲；同时，右拳变掌向身体右下方切掌，掌心向下，力达掌外沿；左掌变拳收抱腰间。目视右掌(图 4-13)。

10.Crouching and palming

(1) Right foot strides a step rightward, squat, at the same time, change right fist into palm and swing it rightward and downward, palm center downward, exert strength to palm edge, change left palm into fist leftward and downward against the waist. Look at right palm (Figure 4-13).

图 4-13(Figure 4-13)

(2)上动不停,右掌变拳回拉收至胸前向右侧前方击肘,肘尖与肩同高。目视肘尖(图4-14)。

(2) Keep moving, change right palm into fist and close it to the front of the chest, swing elbow rightward and forward, elbow tip at the shoulder's level. Look at elbow tip (Figure 4-14).

图 4-14 (Figure 4-14)

(3)上动不停,两脚同时向右碾地,右腿屈膝前弓;同时,右拳变掌向右前上方弹击,掌心向里,掌指向上,力达掌指。目视右掌(图4-15)。

(3) Keep moving, feet grind rightward, bend right knee into the front bow stance, at the same time, change right fist into palm and swing it rightward, for-

ward and upward, palm center inward, fingers upward, exert to fingers. Look at right palm (Figure 4-15).

图 4-15(Figure 4-15)

11.十字弹踢

(1)身体重心移至右腿,屈膝半蹲,左腿向前提膝,脚尖向下;同时,右臂向后屈肘,手腕内旋收至胸前,掌心向上,五指分开;左拳变掌向前插掌,置于右掌上方,掌心向下,五指分开。目视前方(图4-16)。

11.Cross kicking

(1) Shift gravity center to the right leg, bend knees and partly squat, lift left knee forward tiptoes downward, at the same time, close right elbow to the front of the chest, palm center upward, fingers apart, change left fist into palm and swing it forward, to the above of right palm, palm center downward, fingers apart. Look straight ahead (Figure 4-16).

图 4-16(Figure 4-16)

(2)上动不停,左腿向前弹击,脚面绷直,力达脚尖;同时,右掌向下收至胸前,由胸前再展臂向前弹击,力达指尖,掌心向里;左掌随右掌向前弹击的同时向后展臂弹击,掌心向上,力达掌指。目视右掌(图4-17)。

138

(2) Keep moving, right leg kicks forward, keep instep straight, exert to tiptoes, at the same time, close right palm downward to the front of the chest, swing arm forward, exert strength to fingertips, palm inward, make left palm draw curve rightward and forward, and swing it backward, palm center upward, exert to fingers. Look at right palm (Figure 4-17).

图 4-17(Figure 4-17)

12.缩身钳子手

左脚向下收、落至右脚前,两腿屈膝下蹲;同时,左掌经左肩上方向下压掌收于左腿前侧,掌心向左外侧,指尖向下;右掌向下经腹前向上内旋收于左肩前,掌心向左外侧,指尖向上。目视左前上方(图4-18)。

12.Shrinking pliers

Left foot falls in front of right foot, squat, swing left palm upward and downward in front of left leg, palm leftward and outward, fingers apart, fingertips downward, swing right palm downward and upward in front of the abdomen and inward to the front of left shoulder, palm leftward and outward, fingers apart. Look leftward and forward (Figure 4-18).

图 4-18(Figure 4-18)

第二段

Section 2

13.单拍脚

(1)身体上起,左脚向前一步屈膝前弓;同时,左掌变拳,屈肘上提经胸前向前冲出,拳心向下与肩同高;右掌变拳,由胸前向下经腹前收抱腰间。目视左拳(图4-19)。

13.Single foot tapping

(1) Rise, left foot strides a step forward and bend knee into the front bow stance, at the same time, change left palm into fist, bend and lift elbow and swing it in front of the chest, fist center downward at the shoulder's level, change right palm into fist, close it downward in front of the abdomen and against the waist. Look at left fist (Figure 4-19).

图4-19(Figure 4-19)

(2)身体重心向前移至左腿,右脚向前弹击,脚面绷直;同时,右拳变掌,由腰间向体前抢手拍击在右脚脚面上;左拳抱至腰间。目视右脚(图4-20)。

(2) Shift gravity center to left leg, right leg kicks forward, keep instep straight, at the same time, change right fist into palm, swing it forward from the waist to tap right instep, close left fist downward to the waist, tiptoes touchdown. Look at right foot (Figure 4-20).

第四章　少林七星拳

图 4-20（Figure 4-20）

14.左鸡型步

（1）身体向左转身180°，右脚向左脚前下落，左脚脚尖点地，两膝弯曲下蹲，左腿扣在右膝关节后面；同时，右掌变勾手收于胸前向下摆击，勾尖向上贴在身体右侧，左拳变掌向上置于右肩上方，掌指向上。目视左掌（图4-21）。

14.Left constant palming

(1) Turn leftward 180°, right foot falls to the front of left foot, left tiptoes touchdown, squat, close left knee behind right knee, at the same time, change right palm into hook and make it fall, hook tip upward and against the right side, change left fist into palm upward and above right shoulder, fingers upward. Look at left palm (Figure 4-21).

（a）正（Front）　　　（b）反（Back）

图 4-21（Figure 4-21）

（2）上动不停，身体重心移至右腿，左脚向左斜前上方划弧勾踢，置于右腿前，脚尖斜上勾，脚面斜向左外侧，膝与大腿呈水平，右腿屈膝微弯曲下蹲；同时，左掌向下经腹前向身体左下方勾手摆击，置于身体左下侧，勾尖向上；右勾手变掌向上经胸前向身体左上方摆掌，置于左肩上方，掌心向左外

141

侧,掌指向上。目视右掌(图4-22)。

(2) Keep moving, shift gravity center to right leg, make left foot draw curve, hook and kick in front of right leg and obliquely forward, tiptoes obliquely upward, instep obliquely leftward and outward, knees and legs keep horizontal, slightly bend right knee and squat, at the same time, swing left palm leftward and downward from the front of the abdomen to hook and in the leftward and downward, hook tip upward, change right hook into palm and swing it leftward and upward in front of the chest, above the left shoulder, palm leftward and outward, fingers upward. Look at right palm (Figure 4-22).

图 4-22 (Figure 4-22)

15.右鸡型步

左脚向左前下方落步,身体重心移至左腿,屈膝下蹲。右脚向右斜前上方划弧勾踢,置于左腿前,脚尖斜上勾,脚面斜向右外侧,膝与大腿呈水平;同时,右掌向下经腹前向身体右下方勾手摆击,左勾手变掌向右上方摆击置于右肩上方,掌心向右外侧,掌指向上。目视左掌(图4-23)。

15. Right constant palming

Left foot falls leftward and downward, shift gravity center to left leg, slightly squat. Make right foot draw curve, hook and kick from the right side, in front of left leg, tiptoes obliquely upward, instep obliquely rightward and outward, knee and legs keep horizontal, at the same time, swing right palm rightward and downward in front of the abdomen and make it hook, change left hook into palm and swing it rightward and upward and above right shoulder, palm center rightward and outside, fingers upward. Look at left palm (Figure 4-23).

图 4-23(Figure 4-23)

16.左鸡型步

右脚向右前下方落步,身体重心移至右腿,屈膝下蹲,左脚向左斜前上方划弧勾踢,置于右腿前,脚尖斜上勾,脚面斜向左外侧,膝与大腿呈水平,右腿屈膝微弯曲下蹲;同时,左掌向下经腹前向身体左下方勾手摆击,置于身体左下侧,勾尖向上;右勾手变掌向上经胸前向身体左上方摆击,置于左肩上方,掌心向左外侧,掌指向上。目视右掌(图 4-24)。

16.Left constant palming

Right foot falls rightward, forward and downward, shift gravity center to right leg, slightly squat, make left foot draw curve, hook and kick from leftward and obliquely forward, in front of right leg, tiptoes obliquely upward, instep obliquely leftward and outward, knees and legs keep horizontal, bend right leg slightly and squat, at the same time, swing left palm leftward and downward in front of the abdomen and leftward, hook tip upward, change right hook into palm and swing it leftward and upward in front of the chest, above left shoulder, palm center leftward and outward, fingers upward. Look at right palm (Figure 4-24).

图 4-24(Figure 4-24)

17.饿虎势

左脚向前下方落步,屈膝前弓;同时,右掌变拳向下经身体右下方向上摆击置于头部右侧太阳穴前,拳心向下;左勾手变拳向前栽于左膝上,拳心向左外侧,拳眼向里。目视前方(图4-25)。

17.Vigorous palming

Left foot falls forward and downward, bend knee into the front bow stance, at the same time, change right palm into fist and swing it upward and above right shoulder from the right bottom, fist center downward, change left hook into fist against left leg, fist center leftward and outward, fist center inward. Look straight ahead (Figure 4-25).

图 4-25(Figure 4-25)

18.小缩身

(1)身体右转180°,两腿向右碾地,右腿屈膝前弓;同时,右拳向下经胸前向右前方击肘,拳心向下,肘尖与肩同高;左拳向上收抱腰间。目视右前方(图4-26)。

18.Shrinking fist

(1) Turn rightward 180°, legs grind rightward, bend right knee into the front bow stance, at the same time, swing right elbow rightward and forward in front of the chest, fist center downward, elbow tip at the shoulder's level, left fist upward against the waist. Look rightward and forward (Figure 4-26).

(a)正(Front)　　(b)反(Back)

图 4-26(Figure 4-26)

(2)右脚向后撤半步收置于左脚前;两腿屈膝下蹲;同时,右拳变掌向体前下方插掌置于右腿前,掌心向右外侧,指尖向下;左拳变掌向上经胸前向右上方斜插掌置于右肩上方,掌心向右外侧,指尖向上。目视右前上方(图 4-27)。

(2) Right foot retreats half a step to left tiptoes, squat, at the same time, change right fist into palm and swing it forward and downward, in front of right foot, fingers apart, palm center rightward and outward, fingertips downward, change left fist into palm and swing it rightward and upward and above the right shoulder in front of the chest, fingers apart, palm center rightward and outward, fingertips upward. Look rightward, forward and upward (Figure 4-27).

图 4-27(Figure 4-27)

19.十字弹踢

(1)身体重心移至右腿,屈膝半蹲。左腿屈膝上提,脚尖向下;同时,右掌向上至胸前,掌腕顺时针外旋一周,掌心向上,左掌向下置于右掌腕上,掌心向下。目视前方(图 4-28)。

19. Cross kicking

(1) Shift gravity center to the right leg, bend knees and partly squat, lift

left knee, tiptoes downward, at the same time, right palm upward to the front of the chest, wrist turns outward, palm center upward, left palm downward to the right wrist, palm center downward. Look straight ahead (Figure 4-28).

图 4-28(Figure 4-28)

（2）上动不停，左脚向前弹击，脚面绷直，力达脚尖；同时，右掌向下收置胸前，由胸前再展臂向前弹击，力达指尖，掌心向左外侧；左掌随右掌向前弹击的同时，再向后展臂弹击，掌心向左外侧，力达掌指。目视右掌（图 4-29）。

(2) Keep moving, left leg kicks forward, keep instep straight, at the same time, close right palm downward to the front of the chest, swing arm forward, exert strength to fingertips, palm leftward and outward, make left palm draw curve rightward and forward and swing backward, palm leftward and outward, exert to fingers. Look at right palm (Figure 4-29).

图 4-29(Figure 4-29)

20.缩身钳子手

左脚向下收落至右脚前，两腿屈膝下蹲；同时，左掌经左肩上方向下压掌收于左腿前侧，掌心向左外侧，指尖向下；右掌向下经腹前向上内旋收于左肩前，掌心向左外侧，指尖向上。目视左前上方（图 4-30）。

20.Shrinking pliers

Left foot falls in front of right foot, squat, at the same time, swing left palm upward and downward in front of left leg, palm leftward and outward, fingers apart, fingertips downward, swing right palm downward and in front of the abdomen, upward and inward to the front of left shoulder, palm leftward and outward, fingers apart. Look leftward and forward (Figure 4-30).

图 4-30(Figure 4-30)

21.上步一捶

(1)重心移至右腿,右腿屈膝上起,左腿向上提膝,脚尖向下;同时,左掌变拳屈肘向上抱于胸前,拳心向左外侧,拳眼向前下方;右掌变拳向前,向下置于右小臂前下方,拳心向下,转肩含胸。目视左前方(图 4-31)。

21.Striking fist

(1) Lift right leg, bend and lift left knee, tiptoes downward, at the same time, change left palm into fist and close it in front of the chest, palm center leftward and outward, fist center forward and downward, change right palm into fist and swing it forward and downward, fist center downward. Look leftward and forward (Figure 4-31).

图 4-31(Figure 4-31)

(2)上动不停,左脚向前下方落步,屈膝前弓;同时,身体向左拧身,左拳向前方冲击,拳心向下,右拳向下收抱腰间。目视左拳(图4-32)。

(2) Keep moving, left foot falls forward and downward, bend knee and strike forward, at the same time, swing left fist forward, fist center downward, close right fist downward against the waist. Look at left fist (Figure 4-32).

图 4-32(Figure 4-32)

22.又一捶

(1)身体重心向前移至左腿,右腿向上提膝,右脚脚尖向下;同时,右拳向前经胸前收抱于体前,拳心向右外下侧;左拳向后置右小臂前,拳心向下。目视前下方(图4-33)。

22.One more

(1) Shift gravity center forward to left leg, lift right foot, tiptoes downward, at the same time, close right fist against the chest, palm center rightward, outward and downward, left fist backward against right forearm, fist center downward. Look forward and downward (Figure 4-33).

图 4-33(Figure 4-33)

(2)上动不停,右脚向前下落步,屈膝前弓;同时,身体向右拧身,右拳向正前冲出,拳心向下;左拳向下收抱腰间。目视右拳(图4-34)。

(2) Keep moving, right foot falls forward and downward, bend knee into the front bow stance, at the same time, swing right fist forward, fist center downward, left fist downward against the waist. Look at right fist (Figure 4-34).

图4-34(Figure 4-34)

23.再一捶

(1)身体重心向前移至右腿;左腿向上提膝,脚尖向下;同时,左拳向前经胸前收抱于体前,拳心向左外下侧;右拳向后收置左小臂前,拳心向下。目视前下方(图4-35)。

23.Two more

(1) Shift gravity center forward to right leg, lift left knee, tiptoes downward, at the same time, close left fist against the chest, palm center leftward, outward and downward, close right fist backward to left forearm, fist center downward. Look forward and downward (Figure 4-35).

图4-35(Figure 4-35)

(2)上动不停,左腿向前下落步,屈膝前弓;同时,身体向左拧身,左拳向正前冲出,拳心向下,右拳向下收抱腰间。目视左拳(图4-36)。

(2) Keep moving, left leg falls forward, bend knee into the front bow stance, at the same time, swing left fist forward, fist center downward, close right fist downward against the waist. Look at left fist (Figure 4-36).

图4-36(Figure 4-36)

24.缩身钳子手

(1)身体右转180°,两脚向右碾地,右腿屈膝前弓;同时,左拳向下收抱腰间,右臂屈肘上提向前撞击,肘尖与肩同高,拳心向下。目视右前方(图4-37)。

24.Shrinking pliers

(1) Turn rightward 180°, feet grind rightward, bend right knee into the front bow stance, at the same time, close left fist against the waist, bend and lift right elbow and swing it forward, elbow tip at the shoulder's level, fist center downward. Look rightward and forward (Figure 4-37).

图4-37(Figure 4-37)

(2)右脚向后撤半步收置于左脚前,两腿屈膝下蹲;同时,右拳变掌向体前下方插掌置于右腿前,掌心向右外侧,指尖向下;左拳变掌向上经胸前向右上方斜插掌置于右肩上方,掌心向右外侧,指尖向上。目视右前上方(图4-38)。

第四章　少林七星拳

(2) Right foot retreats half a step, to the front of left tiptoes, squat, at the same time, change right fist into palm and swing it forward and downward, to the front of right foot, fingers apart, palm center rightward and outward, fingertips downward, change left fist into palm and swing it upward and rightward, above the right shoulder, fingers apart, palm center rightward and outward, fingertips upward. Look rightward, forward and upward (Figure 4-38).

图 4-38(Figure 4-38)

第三段

Section 3

25.十字弹踢

(1)身体重心移至右腿,屈膝半蹲;左腿屈膝上提,脚尖向下;同时,右掌向上至胸前,掌腕顺时针外旋一周,掌心向上;左掌向下置于右掌腕上,掌心向下。目视前方(图 4-39)。

25.Cross kicking

(1) Shift gravity center to the right leg, bend knees and partly squat, lift left knee, tiptoes downward, at the same time, lift right palm to the chest, swing palm outward, palm center upward, close left palm downward on right wrist, palm center downward. Look straight ahead (Figure 4-39).

图 4-39(Figure 4-39)

151

（2）上动不停，左脚向前弹击，脚面绷直，力达脚尖；同时，右掌向下收置胸前，由胸前再展臂向前弹击，力达指尖，掌心向左外侧；左掌随右掌向前弹击的同时向后展臂弹击，掌心向左外侧，力达掌指。目视右掌（图4-40）。

(2) Keep moving, left leg kicks forward, keep instep straight, at the same time, close right palm to the chest, swing arm forward, exert strength to fingertips, palm center leftward and outward, make left palm draw curve in front of right palm and swing it backward, palm center leftward and outward, exert to fingers. Look at right palm (Figure 4-40).

图4-40(Figure 4-40)

26.缩身钳子手

左脚向下收落至右脚前，两腿屈膝下蹲；同时，左掌经左肩上方向下压掌收于左腿前侧，掌心向左外侧，指尖向下；右掌向下经腹前向上内旋置于左肩前，掌心向左外侧，指尖向上。目视左前上方（图4-41）。

26.Shrinking pliers

Left foot falls in front of right foot, squat, at the same time, swing left palm upward and downward in front of left leg, palm leftward and outward, fingers apart, fingertips downward, swing right palm downward and in front of the abdomen and upward and inward to the front of left shoulder, palm leftward and outward, fingers apart. Look leftward and forward (Figure 4-41).

图4-41(Figure 4-41)

27.护耳掌

左脚向前上一步,屈膝下蹲成马步;同时,左掌向上屈肘由右胸前向左侧外旋摆臂,力达左小臂,掌心斜向上,肘尖向下,右掌向下变拳,收抱腰间。目视左掌(图4-42)。

27.Ear protecting palm

Left foot stride a step forward, squat, at the same time, swing left palm rightward and upward, and leftward via the front of the chest and to the front of left shoulder, palm obliquely upward, change right palm into fist and close it against the waist. Look at left palm (Figure 4-42).

图 4-42(Figure 4-42)

28.拐肘恨鞋

左脚向左碾步,身体左转180°,右脚随身体左转的同时向下震脚,两腿并拢,屈膝下蹲;同时,右臂屈肘随身体左转的同时向左横击肘,置于身体右前方;左掌向下拍击在右小臂上。目视右肘(图4-43)。

28.Cranking and kicking

Left foot grinds leftward, turn leftward 180°, right foot stamps, close legs, squat, at the same time, swing right elbow leftward, close it rightward and forward, left palm pats downward to right forearm. Look at right elbow (Figure 4-43).

图 4-43 (Figure 4-43)

29.外摆莲

身体上起向右转身,右腿随身体右转的力量由里向外摆腿;同时,右拳变掌与左掌同时由身体右侧向左侧(从外向里)依次拍击右脚脚面(外摆莲)。目视两掌(图4-44)。

29.Outward palming

Stand up and turn right, right leg swings outward; at the same time, change right fist into palm and alternately pat right instep with left palm, from right to left (namely swing kicking). Look at palms (Figure 4-44).

图 4-44(Figure 4-44)

30.斜一捶

(1)上动不停,右脚向右下方落步;同时,两掌变拳收抱腰间。目视前方(图4-45)。

30.Oblique punching

(1) Keep moving, right foot falls rightward and downward, at the same time, change palms into fists against the waist. Look straight ahead (Figure 4-45).

图 4-45(Figure 4-45)

第四章 少林七星拳

（2）两脚向右碾地，身体右转，右腿膝前弓成右弓步；同时，左拳由腰间向前冲出，拳心向下，与肩同高；右拳收抱腰间。目视左拳（图4-46）。

(2) Feet grind rightward, turn right, bend right knee into the right bow stance, at the same time, swing left fist forward, fist center downward, at the shoulder's level, close right fist against the waist. Look at left fist (Figure 4-46).

图 4-46（Figure 4-46）

31.下阴捶

（1）身体右转，两脚向左碾地，两腿膝下蹲成马步；同时，左拳向后收拉变掌置于左肩上，掌心斜向上方；右拳抱在腰间。目视右前下方（图4-47）。

31. Crotch fist

(1) Turn right, feet grind leftward, squat, at the same time, close left fist backward and change it into palm on the left shoulder, palm center obliquely upward, hold right fist against the waist. Look right forward and downward (Figure 4-47).

（a）正（Front）　　（b）反（Back）
图 4-47（Figure 4-47）

155

（2）上动不停,右拳由腰间外旋向下冲出,置于右腿外侧,拳心向后。目视右前下方(图4-48)。

(2) Keep moving, swing right fist downward from the waist to right leg outside, palm center backward. Look rightward, forward and downward (Figure 4-48).

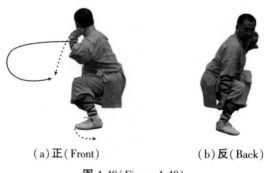

(a)正(Front)　　　(b)反(Back)

图4-48(Figure 4-48)

32.拐肘恨鞋

左脚向左碾步,身体左转90°,右脚随身体左转的同时向下震脚,两腿并拢,膝下蹲;同时,右臂肘随身体左转时向左横击肘,置于身体右前方;左掌向下拍击在右小臂上。目视右肘(图4-49)。

32.Cranking and kicking

Left foot grinds leftward, turn leftward 90°, right foot stamps, close legs, squat, at the same time, lift right elbow and swing it leftward, rightward and forward, left palm center downward and make it pat on the right forearm. Look at right elbow (Figure 4-49).

图4-49(Figure 4-49)

第四章 少林七星拳

33.三崩手

(1)右脚向右一步,两腿膝下蹲成马步;同时,右拳变掌向身体右下方切掌,掌心向下,力达掌外沿;左掌向左下方变拳抱至腰间。目视右掌(图4-50)。

33.Crouching and palming

(1) Right foot strides a step rightward, squat, at the same time, change right fist into palm and swing it rightward and downward, palm center downward, exert strength to palm edge, close left palm leftward and downward, and against the waist. Look at right palm (Figure 4-50).

图 4-50(Figure 4-50)

(2)上动不停,右掌向上回收至胸前,再向右侧前方击肘,肘尖与肩同高。目视肘尖(图 4-51)。

(2) Keep moving, close right palm upward and to the front of the chest, swing elbow rightward and forward, elbow tip at the shoulder's level. Look at elbow tip (Figure 4-51).

图 4-51(Figure 4-51)

(3)上动不停,两脚同时向右碾地,右腿膝前弓;同时,右拳变掌,向右前上方弹击,掌心向里,掌指向上,力达掌指。目视右掌(图4-52)。

(3) Keep moving, feet grind rightward, bend right knee into the front bow stance, at the same time, change right fist into palm, and swing it rightward, forward and upward, palm inward, fingers upward, exert to fingers. Look at right palm (Figure 4-52).

图 4-52(Figure 4-52)

34.十字弹踢

(1)身体重心移至右腿,屈膝半蹲,左腿屈膝上提,脚尖向下;同时,右掌向上至胸前,掌腕顺时针外旋一周,掌心向上;左拳变掌向前插掌,置于右掌腕上,掌心向下,五指分开。目视前方(图4-53)。

34.Cross kicking

(1) Shift gravity center to the right leg, partly squat, lift left knee forward, tiptoes downward, at the same time, lift right palm upward to the front of the chest, swing it outward, palm center upward, change left fist into palm, swing it forward against right palm, palm center downward, fingers apart. Look straight ahead (Figure 4-53).

图 4-53(Figure 4-53)

(2)上动不停,左腿向前弹击,脚面绷直,力达脚尖;同时,右掌向下收置胸前,由胸前再展臂向前弹击,力达指尖,掌心向左外侧;左掌随右掌向前弹击的同时向后展臂弹击,掌心向左外侧,力达掌指。目视右掌(图 4-54)。

(2) Keep moving, left leg kicks forward, keep instep straight, exert to tiptoes, at the same time, close right palm downward to the front of the chest, swing arm forward, exert strength to fingertips, palm center leftward and outward, make left palm draw curve in front of right palm and swing it backward, palm center leftward and outward, exert strength to fingers. Look at right palm (Figure 4-54).

图 4-54(Figure 4-54)

35.缩身钳子手

左脚向下收落至右脚前,两腿膝下蹲;同时,左掌经左肩上方向下压掌收于左腿前侧,掌心向左外侧,指尖向下,右掌向下经腹前向上内旋置于左肩前,掌心向左外侧,指尖向上。目视左前上方(图 4-55)。

35.Shrinking pliers

Left foot falls in front of right foot, squat, at the same time, swing left palm upward and downward in front of left leg, palm center leftward and outward, fingers apart, fingertips downward, swing right palm downward and to the front of the abdomen, upward and swing it inward to the front of left shoulder, palm center leftward and outward, fingers apart. Look leftward and forward (Figure 4-55).

图 4-55(Figure 4-55)

第四段

Section 4

36.二起脚

右脚蹬地,向上跳起并向体前上方弹击,左腿向下自然伸直;同时,左掌向上收抱腰间,右掌由左肩前向下拍击右脚脚面。目视右掌(图 4-56)。

36.Double kicking

Right foot stamps, jump and swing upward, left leg falls and straight, at the same time, close left palm upward and against the waist, make right palm pat right instep from the front of the left shoulder. Look at right palm (Figure 4-56).

图 4-56(Figure 4-56)

37.双按掌

(1)上动不停,身体左转 180°向下落地,右脚落地的同时向下震脚,左脚随即蹬地提膝;同时,两臂分别向身体两侧摆击,掌心向上与肩同高。目视前下方(图 4-57)。

37.Double palming

(1) Keep moving, right foot falls and stamps, turn leftward 180°, at the same time, left foot stamps, lift knee, at the same time, swing arms to both sides, palm centers upward and at the shoulder's level. Look forward and downward (Figure 4-57).

图 4-57（Figure 4-57）

（2）上动不停，左腿向身体左侧下方落步，右腿膝下蹲成仆步；同时，两掌由上向下经胸前向体前下方按掌，掌心向下，两掌掌指相对。目视两掌（图 4-58）。

（2）Keep moving, left leg falls to the leftward, at the same time, right leg squats into the left drop stance, at the same time, close palms downward to the front of the chest, press it forward and downward, palm center downward, fingers against each other. Look at palms (Figure 4-58).

图 4-58（Figure 4-58）

38.双撑肘

身体上起，双脚向左碾地，左腿膝前弓；同时，两掌变拳，两臂上提屈肘向身体两侧夹击，拳心向上。目视右拳（图 4-59）。

38.Double elbowing

Rise, bend left knee, at the same time, change palms into fists, lift arms and close elbows to strike to both sides, fist center upward. Look at right fist (Figure 4-59).

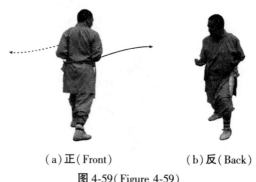

(a)正(Front)　　(b)反(Back)

图 4-59(Figure 4-59)

39.十字通背

上动不停,两拳分别向身体两侧冲出,拳心向下,与肩同高。目视右拳(图4-60)。

39.Cross punching

Keep moving, fists punch to both sides, fist centers downward and at the shoulder's level. Look at right fist (Figure 4-60).

图 4-60(Figure 4-60)

40.小缩身

右脚向左脚前收步,两腿膝下蹲;同时,右拳变掌向下、向上经胸前向左肩前插掌,掌心向左外侧,五指分开,指尖向上;左拳变掌向前、向下经左肩前下插掌,置于左腿前;掌心向左外侧,指尖向下。目视左前方(图4-61)。

40.Shrinking fist

Close right foot in front of left foot, squat, at the same time, change right fist into palm and swing it downward and upward via the front of the chest and to the front of the left shoulder, palm center leftward and outward, fingers apart, fingertips upward, change left fist into palm and swing it forward and downward via the front of the chest and to the front of left leg, palm center leftward and outward, fingers apart, fingertips downward. Look leftward and forward (Figure 4-61).

图 4-61(Figure 4-61)

41.上步一捶

左脚向前上一步,左腿屈膝前弓;同时,左掌变拳向上由胸前向体前冲出,拳心向下,与肩同高;右掌变拳向下经胸前收抱腰间。目视左拳(图 4-62)。

41.Striking fist

Left leg strides a step forward, bend left knee into the front bow stance, at the same time, change left palm into fist and swing it forward from the front of the chest, fist center downward and at the shoulder's level, change right palm into fist downward and close it against the waist. Look at left fist (Figure 4-62).

图 4-62(Figure 4-62)

42.又一捶

右脚向前一步,膝前弓;同时,右拳向体前冲出,拳心向下,与肩同高;左拳向后收抱腰间。目视右拳(图4-63)。

42.One more

Right foot strides a step forward, bend knee into the front bow stance, at the same time, swing right fist forward, fist center downward and at the shoulder's level, Close left fist backward and against the waist. Look at right fist (Figure 4-63).

图 4-63(Figure 4-63)

43.转身十字手

(1)两脚向左碾地,身体左转,左拳变掌向后上架于头顶上方;同时,右拳收抱腰间。目视左掌(图4-64)。

43.Turning and crossing

(1) Feet grind leftward, turn left, change left fist into palm and close it overhead, at the same time, close right fist against the waist. Look at left palm (Figure 4-64).

图 4-64(Figure 4-64)

(2)身体左转180°,右腿随身体左转的同时向上提膝;左掌翻腕下旋按于体前,掌心向下,右拳变掌向头顶上方摆击。目视左掌(图 4-65)。

(2) Turn left 180°. Right knee lifts at the same time. Left palm twists and presses forward, palm center downward. Change right fist into palm and swings overhead. Look at left palm (Figure 4-65).

图 4-65(Figure 4-65)

(3)上动不停,右脚向右下方落步,两腿膝下蹲;同时,右掌向下插掌于腹前,掌心向右外侧,五指分开,指尖向下;左掌内旋向上插掌置于体前上方,掌心向右外侧,五指分开,指尖向上。目视正前方,同时,发出"威"的声音(图 4-66)。

(3) Keep moving, right foot galls rightward and downward, squat, at the same time, swing right palm downward to the front of abdomen, palm center rightward and outward, fingers apart, fingertips downward, swing left palm inward and upward, palm center rightward and outward, fingers apart, fingertips upward. Look straight ahead, at the same time cry "Wei" (Figure 4-66).

图 4-66(Figure 4-66)

44.收势

(1)身体上起,左脚向右脚处并拢,两掌变拳收抱腰间。目视前方(图

4-67)。

44.Closing

(1) Stand up, close left foot to right foot, change palms into fists and against the waist. Look straight ahead (Figure 4-67).

图 4-67(Figure 4-67)

(2)两拳变掌向下垂于身体两侧,成立正姿势。目视前方(图 4-68)。

(2) Change fists into palms, and make them naturally hang into standing at attention. Look straight ahead (Figure 4-68).

图 4-68(Figure 4-68)

第五章　少林单刀
Chapter 5　Shaolin Single Broadsword

第一节　套路动作名称
Quarter 1　Routine Name

第一段
Section 1

1. 预备势（Preparation）
2. 弓步抱刀冲拳（Bow stance broadsword punching）
3. 裹脑虚步藏刀（Right-shoulder to left-shoulder empty stance broadsword hiding）
4. 缠头劈刀（Left-shoulder to right-shoulder broadsword chopping）
5. 虚步藏刀（Empty stance broadsword hiding）
6. 弓步刺刀（Bow stance broadsword stabbing）
7. 并步下扫刀（Step touch broadsword sweeping）
8. 歇步藏刀（Sitting stance broadsword hiding）
9. 虚步藏刀（Empty stance broadsword hiding）
10. 左弓步斩刀（Left bow stance broadsword cutting）
11. 右弓步推刀（Right bow stance broadsword pushing）
12. 左弓步斩刀（Left bow stance broadsword cutting）
13. 轮臂刺刀（Arm waving broadsword stabbing）
14. 提膝立刀（Knee lifting broadsword erecting）
15. 弓步下栽刀（Bow stance broadsword plunging）
16. 背后藏刀（Back broadsword hiding）

第二段

Section 2

17. 弓步托刀（Bow stance broadsword supporting）
18. 仆步按刀（Drop stance broadsword pressing）
19. 上推刀（Broadsword upward pushing）
20. 下撩刀（Broadsword downward thrusting）
21. 蹲步下劈刀（Squatting broadsword chopping）
22. 震脚上崩刀（Stamping and broadsword upward hitting）
23. 虚步藏刀（Empty stance broadsword hiding）
24. 提膝后背刀（Knee lifting and broadsword backing）
25. 左歇步斩刀（Left sitting stance broadsword cutting）
26. 右歇步劈刀（Right sitting stance broadsword chopping）
27. 跃步下劈刀（Galloping broadsword chopping）
28. 腾空外摆抹刀（Broadsword outward swaying and wiping）

第三段

Section 3

29. 箭弹刺刀（Spring broadsword stabbing）
30. 弓步背刀（Bow stance broadsword backing）
31. 三劈刀（Three broadsword chopping）
32. 马步背刀（Horse-riding stance broadsword backing）
33. 旋风脚马步背刀（Whirlwind kicking horse-riding stance broadsword backing）
34. 绞刀提膝（Broadsword twisting and knee lifting）
35. 回头望月刀（Back leg kicking broadsword）

第四段

Section 4

36. 马步磨盘刀（Horse-riding stance millstone broadsword）
37. 单拍脚虚步藏刀（Single batting empty stance broadsword hiding）
38. 蹲步抱刀（Squatting and broadsword tackling）
39. 二起飞脚（Double flying and kicking）

40.马步架拳抱刀(Horse-riding stance broadsword tackling)

41.并步抱刀(Step touch broadsword tackling)

42.收势(Closing)

第二节 套路动作图解
Quarter 2 Figures of Routine Movements

第一段
Section 1

1.预备势

(1)两脚并立,左手抱刀垂于身体左侧,右臂自然下垂,五指并拢,贴于腿侧。目视前方(图5-1)。

1.Preparation

(1)Feet parallel, left hand holds broadsword leftward, right arm falls naturally, close fingers against the leg. Look straight ahead(Figure 5-1).

图5-1(Figure 5-1)

(2)上动不停,两手上提抱于腰间。右手变拳,目视前方(图5-2)。

(2)Keep moving, lift hands against the waist. Change right hand into fist, Look straight ahead(Figure 5-2).

图 5-2（Figure 5-2）

2.弓步抱刀冲拳

（1）身体重心稍左移,右脚提起向下震脚,左膝向上提起；同时,左手持刀向右腹前摆击,刀刃向上,刀尖向左。目视刀尖（图 5-3）。

2.Bow stance broadsword punching

（1）Shift gravity center slightly leftward, lift right foot and make it stamp, left knee, at the same time, left hand swings broadsword forward and rightward, broadsword blade upward, broadsword point leftward. Look at broadsword tip (Figure 5-3).

图 5-3（Figure 5-3）

（2）上动不停,身体左转 90°左脚向前下落,成左弓步；左手握刀向左平摆划弧抱于腰间,刀刃向前,刀尖向上。右拳向前冲出,高与肩平。目视前方（图 5-4）。

（2）Keep moving, turn leftward 90°, left foot falls forward and downward into the left bow stance, left hand swings broadsword leftward and draw curve against the waist, broadsword blade forward, broadsword point upward. Right fist forward, keep at the shoulder's level. Look straight ahead (Figure 5-4).

图 5-4(Figure 5-4)

3.裹脑虚步藏刀

(1)身体右转,右脚蹬地,腾空跳起;两臂由头顶上方向下、向右绕头划弧于体前,右手接刀,左手向下附于右手臂处(图 5-5)。

3.Right-shoulder to left-shoulder empty stance broadsword hiding

(1)Turn right, feet fall, jump, and arms draw curve overhead and rightward, right hand picks broadsword, left hand downward and against right arm (Figure 5-5).

图 5-5(Figure 5-5)

(2)上动不停,左脚先落地,右脚随即落地,身体右转 90°成左弓步;右手握刀,左掌附于刀柄上。目视右手(图 5-6)。

(2)Keep moving, left foot falls and right foot falls, turn rightward 90° into the left bow stance, right hand holds broadsword, left palm against broadsword handle. Look at right hand (Figure 5-6).

图 5-6(Figure 5-6)

（3）上动不停，身体左转90°，左脚向后收于右腿内侧，脚尖点地，两腿屈膝下蹲成左丁步；同时，两臂向右摆击置于身体右上方，右手持刀左掌置于右手臂内侧，掌心向外。目视左前方（图5-7）。

(3) Keep moving, turn leftward 90°, close left foot backward and into right leg inward, tiptoes touchdown, bend knees and squat into the left T-step, at the same time, arms swing rightward and upward, right hand holds broadsword, left palm against right arm inward, palm center outward. Look leftward (Figure 5-7).

图5-7（Figure 5-7）

4.缠头劈刀

（1）左脚向前一步，身体左转180°，右腿向上提膝；同时，右手持刀经头顶从左肩外侧向后绕刀，刀尖斜向下；左掌向下摆击至左胸前，掌心向右，掌指向上。目视左下方（图5-8）。

4. Left-shoulder to right-shoulder broadsword chopping

(1) Turn leftward 180°, left foot strides one step forward, lift right knee, at the same time, right hand swings broadsword backward via overhead and left shoulder outward, broadsword tip obliquely downward, swing left palm to the left chest, palm rightward, fingers upward. Look leftward and downward (Figure 5-8).

图5-8（Figure 5-8）

（2）上动不停，右脚向右前方落步，两腿屈膝下蹲成马步；同时，右手持刀向身体右侧下劈刀，刀刃斜向下；左掌置于右手臂肘关节处。目视右前下方（图5-9）。

(2) Keep moving, right foot falls rightward and forward, bend knees and squat into the horse-riding stance, at the same time, right hand swings broadsword rightward and downward, broadsword blade obliquely downward, left palm against right elbow joints. Look rightward, forward and downward (Figure 5-9).

图 5-9(Figure 5-9)

5.虚步藏刀

身体重心稍向左移，左脚蹬地跳起，身体右转180°，右脚向后落步，左脚向前垫步下落成左虚步；同时，右手持刀，手腕放松向下、向上划弧一周置于体前，刀尖向上，刀刃向前，左掌置于右手腕上。目视刀尖（图5-10）。

5. Empty stance broadsword hiding

Shift gravity center slightly leftward, left foot falls and jumps, turn rightward 180°, right foot retreats and falls, left foot falls forward into the left empty stance, at the same time, right hand holds broadsword, loosen wrist, swing downward and upward to draw curve a circle, broadsword tip upward, broadsword blade forward, left palm against the right wrist. Look at broadsword tip (Figure 5-10).

图 5-10(Figure 5-10)

6.弓步刺刀

左脚向前移半步,成左弓步;同时,右手持刀向前刺刀,刀尖向前,刀刃向下,左掌置于右小臂内侧。目视刀尖(图5-11)。

6. Bow stance broadsword stabbing

Left foot strides half a step forward into the left bow stance, at the same time, right hand stabs broadsword forward, broadsword tip forward, broadsword blade downward, and left palm against in the right forearm inward. Look at broadsword tip (Figure 5-11).

图5-11(Figure 5-11)

7.并步下扫刀

身体右转90°,左脚向后收步与右脚并拢下蹲;同时,右手持刀外旋向右下扫刀;左掌向上摆击,左臂与右臂成一条直线,掌心向上。目视刀尖(图5-12)。

7. Step touch broadsword sweeping

Turn rightward 90°, retreat left foot backward and close it against right foot, at the same time, right hand swings broadsword outward, rightward and downward, left palm swing upward, left arm and right arm in a straight line, palm center upward. Look at broadsword tip (Figure 5-12).

图5-12(Figure 5-12)

第五章 少林单刀

8.歇步藏刀

(1)身体重心移至右腿,左腿向上提膝,右手持刀向上挑刀;同时,左掌向上摆击,与肩同高。目视右前方(图5-13)。

8. Sitting stance broadsword hiding

(1) Lift left knee, right hand picks broadsword upward, at the same time, left palm swings upward, keep at the shoulder's level. Look rightward and forward (Figure 5-13).

图5-13(Figure 5-13)

(2)上动不停,左脚向右腿前下方落步两腿屈膝下蹲成歇步;同时,右手持刀由下向左经体前向上穿刀,左掌向下、向上、向右摆掌附于右肩前方,掌心向右,掌指向上。目视刀尖(图5-14)。

(2) Keep moving, left foot falls rightward forward and downward into the sitting stance, at the same time, right hand swings broadsword leftward and upward, left palm against right shoulder forward, palm center rightward, fingers upward. Look at broadsword tip (Figure 5-14).

图5-14(Figure 5-14)

9.虚步藏刀

(1)身体右转180°,右手持刀向下经体前向右前方劈刀,刀尖向上,左掌向右上方摆击,掌心向左。目随刀走(图5-15)。

9. Empty stance broadsword hiding

(1) Turn rightward 180°, right hand chops broadsword rightward, forward, broadsword tip upward, left palm swings rightward and upward, palm center leftward. Look at broadsword (Figure 5-15).

图 5-15(Figure 5-15)

(2)上动不停,左脚蹬地跳起,向前落步,右脚后退半步成左虚步;同时,右手持刀,刀尖向下、向左、向上、向下划圆收于体前,左掌向下收置于右手腕上。目视刀尖(图5-16)。

(2) Keep moving, left foot kicks and jumps, falls forward, right foot retreats half a step into the left empty stance, at the same time, right hand holds broadsword, swing broadsword tip downward, leftward, upward, and downward and draw a circle, left palm downward against right wrist. Look at broadsword tip (Figure 5-16).

图 5-16(Figure 5-16)

第五章　少林单刀

10.左弓步斩刀

（1）身体重心移至右腿,左腿屈膝上提;同时,右手持刀外旋经左臂外侧向后绕刀,刀刃向左,刀尖向下;左掌向前、向上划弧。目视前方(图5-17)。

10. Left bow stance broadsword cutting

(1) Shift gravity center backward, bend and lift left knee, at the same time, right hand swings broadsword outward and backward via left arm outward, broadsword blade leftward, broadsword tip downward, left palm forward, draw curve upward. Look straight ahead (Figure 5-17).

图 5-17(Figure 5-17)

（2）上动不停,左脚向左前方45°下落成左弓步;同时,右手持刀外旋向下、向右、向前由腰间向左上方45°斩刀,刀刃向前,刀尖向右;左掌附在右手腕上。目视刀尖(图5-18)。

(2) Keep moving, left foot falls leftward and forward 45° into the left bow stance, at the same time, right hand swings broadsword outward, downward, rightward and forward, and leftward and upward 45° from the waist, broadsword blade forward, broadsword tip rightward, left palm against right wrist. Look at broadsword tip (Figure 5-18).

图 5-18(Figure 5-18)

177

11.右弓步推刀

(1)右腿向前屈膝提起;同时,右手持刀内旋向下、向后、向前绕刀,刀刃向前,刀尖向左。左臂随刀向绕刀时向左摆臂再向下、向上划弧一周置于右手腕上。目视前方(图5-19)。

11. Right bow stance broadsword pushing

(1) Bend and lift right knee, at the same time, right hand swings broadsword downward, backward and forward, broadsword blade forward, broadsword tip leftward. Look straight ahead (Figure 5-19).

图5-19(Figure 5-19)

(2)上动不停,右脚向右前方45°落步成右弓步;同时,右手持刀向体前45°方向推刀,刀刃向前,刀尖向左;左手置于右手腕上。目视前方(图5-20)。

(2) Keep moving, right foot falls rightward and forward 45° into the bow stance, at the same time, right hand pushes broadsword forward 45°, broadsword blade forward, broadsword tip leftward, left hand against right wrist. Look straight ahead (Figure 5-20).

图5-20(Figure 5-20)

12.左弓步斩刀

(1)身体重心前移至右腿,左腿屈膝提起;同时,右手持刀向上绕于左肩后,刀尖向下;左掌向上摆击置于右手腕上。目视前方(图5-21)。

12. Left bow stance broadsword cutting

(1) Shift gravity center forward, bend and lift left knee, at the same time, right hand swings broadsword upward and behind left shoulder, broadsword tip downward, swing left palm upward. Look straight ahead (Figure 5-21).

图 5-21(Figure 5-21)

(2)上动不停,左脚向左前45°下落成左弓步;同时,右手持刀向前45°方向斩刀。左掌向下收于腰间后,再向前置于右手腕上。目视刀尖(图5-22)。

(2) Keep moving, left foot falls forward and forward 45° into the left bow stance, at the same time, right hand cuts broadsword forward 45°. Left palm against right wrist. Look at broadsword tip (Figure 5-22).

图 5-22(Figure 5-22)

13.轮臂刺刀

(1)两脚向右碾地,身体向右转;同时,右手持刀向上、向后、向下绕刀;

左掌向左摆击,掌心向左前方。目视刀尖(图 5-23)。

13. Arm waving broadsword stabbing

(1) Turn rightward, at the same time, right hand swings broadsword upward, backward and downward, left palm leftward, palm center leftward and forward. Look at broadsword tip (Figure 5-23).

图 5-23(Figure 5-23)

(2)上动不停,两脚向右碾地,身体继续向右后方转 90°再迅速向左前方转 270°;同时,右手持刀向后、向上、向右、向下、向左上方绕刀;左臂随身体摆动,由上向下、向上置于身体左侧。目随刀走(图 5-24)。

(2) Keep moving, turn rightward and backward 90° and leftward and forward 270°, at the same time, right hand swings broadsword backward, upward, rightward, downward, and leftward and upward, left arm downward, upward and leftward. Look at broadsword (Figure 5-24).

图 5-24(Figure 5-24)

(3)上动不停,身体右转 90°;同时,右手持刀向上挑刀,刀背贴在右肩上,刀刃向上,刀尖向后。左掌向前置于刀柄上。目视刀尖(图 5-25)。

(3) Keep moving, turn rightward 90°, at the same time, right hand picks

broadsword upward, broadsword back against right shoulder, broadsword blade upward, broadsword tip backward, left palm forward against broadsword handle. Look at broadsword tip (Figure 5-25).

图 5-25(Figure 5-25)

（4）上动不停，两脚向右碾地，身体右转90°成右弓步；同时，右手持刀，手腕内旋向后刺刀，刀刃向下；左掌向左摆击，与肩同高，掌心向后。目视刀尖(图5-26)。

（4）Keep moving, feet grind rightward, turn rightward 90° into the right bow stance, at the same time, right hand holds broadsword, wrist turns inward stabs broadsword backward, broadsword blade downward, left palm swings leftward, keep at the shoulder's level, palm center backward. Look at broadsword tip (Figure 5-26).

图 5-26(Figure 5-26)

14.提膝立刀

身体重心前移至右腿，左腿向前屈膝上提；同时，右手持刀从右腿外侧向下、向上绕转一周置于体前，刀刃向前，刀尖向上。左掌向前置于右手背上。目视前方(图5-27)。

14. Knee lifting broadsword erecting

Shift gravity center to right leg, bend and lift left leg, at the same time, right hand swings broadsword downward, upward to turn a circle from right leg outward, broadsword blade forward, broadsword tip upward, left palm forward against right wrist inward. Look straight ahead (Figure 5-27).

图 5-27(Figure 5-27)

15.弓步下栽刀

左脚向前下落成左弓步;同时,右手持刀向下、向后、向上经头顶向前下方刺刀,刀尖斜向下;左掌随刀下劈时向下、向上摆掌置于右手腕上。目视前方(图 5-28)。

15. Bow stance broadsword plunging

Left foot falls forward and downward into the left bow stance, at the same time, right hand stabs broadsword downward, backward and upward, forward and downward, broadsword tip downward, left palm against right wrist. Look straight ahead (Figure 5-28).

图 5-28(Figure 5-28)

第五章 少林单刀

16.背后藏刀

身体右转90°,左脚向后收于右脚内侧,脚尖点地,两腿下蹲成丁字步;同时,右手持刀向下、向后在背后劈刀划弧绕约一周,刀身贴于身体背部,刀刃向左前,刀尖向上;左掌随身体右转向下收置于右肩前,掌心向后。目视左前方(图5-29)。

16. Back broadsword hiding

Turn rightward 90°, close left foot backward in right foot inward, tiptoes touchdown, squat into the T-stance, at the same time, right hand swings broadsword backward, downward and outward a circle, broadsword against the back, broadsword blade forward and leftward, broadsword tip upward, left palm against right shoulder, palm center backward. Look leftward (Figure 5-29).

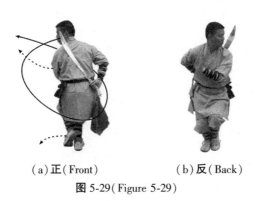

(a)正(Front)　　(b)反(Back)

图 5-29(Figure 5-29)

第二段

Section 2

17.弓步托刀

(1)左脚向前半步成左虚步;同时,右手持刀内旋从身体后侧经腹前向体前上方推刀,刀刃斜向上,刀尖斜向下。左掌向前附在刀背上。目视前方(图5-30)。

17.Bow stance broadsword supporting

(1) Left foot strides half a step into the left empty stance, at the same

183

time, right hand pushes broadsword to the front of the abdomen from behind, broadsword blade obliquely upward, broadsword tip slantingly downward, left palm against broadsword back. Look straight ahead (Figure 5-30).

图 5-30(Figure 5-30)

（2）上动不停，左脚向前上半步成左弓步；同时，右手持刀向左前方推刀，左掌附于刀背上。目视前方（图5-31）。

(2) Keep moving, left foot strides one step into the left bow stance, at the same time, right hand pushes broadsword leftward and forward, left palm against the broadsword back. Look straight ahead (Figure 5-31).

图 5-31(Figure 5-31)

18.仆步按刀

（1）身体重心向前移至左腿，右腿屈膝提膝；同时，右手持刀向上托刀，左掌附于刀背上。目视刀尖（图5-32）。

18. Drop stance broadsword pressing

(1) Shift gravity center to left leg, bend and lift right knee, at the same time, right hand holds broadsword upward, left palm against broadsword back.

Look at broadsword tip (Figure 5-32).

图 5-32 (Figure 5-32)

（2）上动不停，左脚向前蹬地跳起，右腿自然下垂；同时，右手持刀向头顶右上方带刀，左掌附在刀背上。目视右手（图5-33）。

(2) Keep moving, left foot falls and jumps, right leg naturally falls, at the same time, right hand swings broadsword overhead, left palm against broadsword back. Look at right hand (Figure 5-33).

图 5-33 (Figure 5-33)

（3）右脚落地，左腿向前落步，右腿屈膝下蹲成仆步；同时，右手持刀向右、向下划弧按刀于腹前，刀刃向下。左掌按在刀背上。目视右手（图5-34）。

(3) Right foot falls, left leg falls into to the drop stance, at the same time, right hand draws curve rightward and downward in front of the abdomen, broadsword blade downward, left palm against broadsword back. Look at broadsword

tip (Figure 5-34).

图 5-34(Figure 5-34)

19.上推刀

身体上起重心向前移至左腿,右脚向前收于左脚内侧并屈膝向下震脚;同时,右手持刀屈肘向上翻腕收刀至胸前,刀刃向上、向头顶上方推刀,左掌附于刀背上。目视前方(图 5-35)。

19. Broadsword upward pushing

Shift gravity center to left leg, close right foot forward, bend left knee downward and make it stamp, at the same time, right hand pushes broadsword overhead from the front of the chest, left palm against the broadsword back. Look straight ahead (Figure 5-35).

图 5-35(Figure 5-35)

20.下撩刀

(1)左脚掌向左碾地,身体左转 180°,右脚向前上步成右弓步;同时,右手持刀由下向右上方撩刀;左掌随身体左转的同时向后摆击,掌心向后。目视刀尖(图 5-36)。

20. Broadsword downward thrusting

(1) Left sole grinds leftward, turn leftward 180°, right foot strides one step into the right bow stance, at the same time, right hand thrusts broadsword rightward and upward, left palm swings backward, palm center backward. Look at broadsword tip (Figure 5-36).

图 5-36(Figure 5-36)

(2)上动不停,身体继续左转 90°,左脚经右腿后向右后插步,脚尖点地;同时,右手持刀手腕内旋划弧向下经腹前向左下方撩刀,刀刃斜向上;左掌向下经腹前向左上方摆击,掌心向上。目视刀尖(图 5-37)。

(2) Keep moving, turn leftward 90°, left foot strides rightward and backward via right leg, tiptoes touchdown, at the same time, right hand thrusts broadsword leftward and downward in front of the abdomen, broadsword blade obliquely upward, left palm swings leftward and upward in front of the abdomen, supinely. Look at broadsword tip (Figure 5-37).

图 5-37 (Figure 5-37)

21.蹲步下劈刀

(1)身体向右翻腰;同时,右手持刀向右、向上绞刀,刀尖斜向右下方,左掌左摆架于头顶。目视左掌(图 5-38)。

21. Squatting broadsword chopping

(1) Turn waist rightward, at the same time, right hand swings broadsword rightward and upward, broadsword tip obliquely rightward and downward, left palm against overhead. Look at left palm (Figure 5-38).

图 5-38(Figure 5-38)

(2)上动不停,身体继续左转 90°,右脚向前一步同左脚并拢向下震脚,两腿屈膝下蹲;同时,右手持刀外旋向上、向前、向下劈刀;左掌向下摆击于腹前向上收置于右小臂内侧。目视刀尖(图 5-39)。

(2) Keep moving, turn leftward 90°, close right foot forward to left foot inward and make it stamp, at the same time, right hand chops broadsword outward, upward, forward and downward, left palm against right forearm inward. Look at broadsword tip (Figure 5-39).

图 5-39(Figure 5-39)

第五章 少林单刀

22.震脚上崩刀

(1)身体重心移至左脚,右腿屈膝上提;同时,右手持刀向下经右腿外侧(右臂摆动与身体成45°)向后拉刀,左掌向前摆击。目视左掌(图5-40)。

22. Stamping and broadsword upward hitting

(1) Shift gravity center to the left foot, bend and lift right knee, at the same time, right hand pulls broadsword backward to right leg outward (swing right arm 45°), left palm swings forward. Look at left palm (Figure 5-40).

图5-40(Figure 5-40)

(2)上动不停,右腿向下屈膝震脚,右手持刀经身体右侧向前、向上崩刀;刀刃向前,刀尖向上,左掌向下附于右手腕上。目视刀尖(图5-41)。

(2) Keep moving, right foot stamps, right hand swings broadsword forward and upward from rightward, broadsword blade forward, broadsword tip upward, left palm downward and against right wrist. Look at broadsword tip (Figure 5-41).

图5-41(Figure 5-41)

23.虚步藏刀

(1)右脚向前上一步,身体左转90°,两腿屈膝自然下蹲;右手持刀向上缠头一周后向左平扫刀,刀刃向左。左掌随刀向后缠头时向体侧摆击,向下收在右手腕上。目视刀尖(图5-42)。

23. Empty stance broadsword hiding

(1) Right foot strides one step, turn leftward 90°, bend knees and squat, right hand swings broadsword leftward, broadsword blade leftward, left palm against right wrist. Look at broadsword tip (Figure 5-42).

图 5-42(Figure 5-42)

(2)上动不停,右脚蹬地,身体右转360°;同时,右手持刀向右经后背绕左肩裹脑平扫,左掌随身体腾空向身体左侧摆击(图5-43)。

(2) Keep moving, feet fall, turn rightward 360°, at the same time, right hand swings broadsword outward via the back and left shoulder, jump and left palm swings leftward (Figure 5-43).

图 5-43(Figure 5-43)

(3)上动不停,右脚落地,左脚随即落下;右腿屈膝半蹲,左脚尖点地成左虚步;同时,右手持刀向下经腹前向后拉刀至身体右下方;左掌向前推掌。目视前方(图5-44)。

(3) Keep moving, right foot falls and left foot falls, bend right knee on semi-crouch balance, left tiptoes touchdown into the left empty stance, at the same time, right hand swings broadsword rightward and downward in front of the abdomen, left palm pushes forward. Look straight ahead (Figure 5-44).

图 5-44(Figure 5-44)

24.提膝后背刀

(1)右手持刀,经右腿外侧向前、向后绕刀于身体左侧,刀尖斜向下,刀刃斜向左前下方,左掌回收向下附于右小臂下方,掌心向外,掌指向上。目视右手(图 5-45)。

24. Knee lifting and broadsword backing

(1) Right hand swings broadsword forward and backward via right leg outward and the left side, broadsword tip slantly downward, broadsword blade obliquely leftward, forward and downward, left palm against right forearm, palm center outward, fingers upward. Look at right hand (Figure 5-45).

图 5-45(Figure 5-45)

(2)上动不停,身体重心移至右脚,左脚向上提起成左提膝式;同时,右手持刀向上、向后绕刀,刀背贴于身体背部,左掌向身体左侧变勾手摆击,微高于肩。目视前方(图 5-46)。

(2) Keep moving, lift and straighten left instep, at the same time, right hand swings broadsword upward and backward, broadsword back against the back, left palm hooks leftward, slightly higher than shoulders. Look straight ahead (Figure 5-46).

图 5-46(Figure 5-46)

25.左歇步斩刀

身体左转90°,左脚尖下落外展,两腿屈膝下蹲成左歇步;同时,右手持刀向下斩刀,刀刃向前,刀尖向上。左手变掌向下收掌附于右手臂内侧。目视前方(图 5-47)。

25. Left sitting stance broadsword cutting

Turn leftward 90°, left tiptoes outreach and fall, bend knees and squat into the left sitting stance, at the same time, right hand cuts broadsword downward, broadsword blade forward, broadsword tip upward. Change left hand into palm against right arm inward. Look straight ahead (Figure 5-47).

图 5-47(Figure 5-47)

第五章 少林单刀

26.右歇步劈刀

（1）身体上起，两脚向右碾地，身体左转90°，右脚向前一步，右手持刀向下、向后、向上抢劈，刀刃向上，刀尖向后；同时，左掌向左、向上附于右手腕上。目视前方（图5-48）。

26. Right sitting stance broadsword chopping

（1）Arise, right foot strides one step, turn leftward 90°, right hand swings broadsword downward, backward and upward, broadsword blade upward, broadsword tip backward, at the same time, left palm leftward, upward and against right wrist. Look straight ahead (Figure 5-48).

图5-48（Figure 5-48）

（2）上动不停，两脚掌向右碾地，身体向右转180°，两腿屈膝下蹲成右歇步；同时，右手持刀向前、向下劈刀，刀刃斜向下，刀尖斜向上，左掌附在右手腕上。目视刀尖（图5-49）。

（2）Keep moving, sole grinds rightward, turn rightward 180°, bend knees and squat into the right sitting stance, at the same time, right hand chops broadsword forward and downward, broadsword blade obliquely downward, broadsword tip slantly upward, left palm against right wrist. Look at broadsword tip (Figure 5-49).

图5-49（Figure 5-49）

193

27.跃步下劈刀

(1)身体上起,右脚向前上半步用力蹬地向上跳起,左腿向前提膝;同时,右手持刀向下经体前向右上方撩刀,左掌向身体左侧摆动,与肩同高。目视左前下方(图 5-50)。

27. Galloping broadsword chopping

(1) Right foot strides half a step and jump, lift leg knee forward, at the same time, right hand cuts broadsword downward, rightward and upward, left palm swingings leftward, keep at the shoulder's level. Look leftward, forward and downward (Figure 5-50).

图 5-50(Figure 5-50)

(2)上动不停,左腿先落地,右腿向左腿后插步下落,两腿屈膝下蹲成左歇步;同时,右手持刀,手臂外旋向上经头顶再向下劈刀于体侧,目视刀刃(图 5-51)。

(2) Keep moving, legs fall, right leg against left leg inward, bend knees and squat into the left sitting stance, at the same time, right hand chops broadsword downward, arm swings outward, Look at broadsword blade (Figure 5-51).

图 5-51 (Figure 5-51)

28.腾空外摆抹刀

(1)身体右转180°,两腿屈膝成蹲步;同时,右手持刀随身体右转的旋力向下扫刀,左掌附于刀背上。目视刀尖(图5-52)。

28. Broadsword outward swaying and wiping

(1) Turn rightward 180° and squat, at the same time, right hand sweeps broadsword downward a circle to the front of right foot, left palm against broadsword back. Look at broadsword tip (Figure 5-52).

图 5-52(Figure 5-52)

(2)上动不停,身体继续右转180°,左脚向右上一步,两腿下蹲成蹲步;同时,右手持刀随身体右转的力量向下平扫刀。目视刀尖(图5-53)。

(2) Keep moving, turn rightward 180°, left foot strides one step rightward, squat, at the same time, right hand sweeps broadsword rightward. Look at left hand (Figure 5-53).

图 5-53(Figure 5-53)

(3)上动不停,右脚蹬地,身体腾空向右后转体270°,右腿由左向右侧腾空摆击,左腿自然下垂;同时,右手持刀由右向左绕裹脑绕刀,刀刃向上,刀尖向后。左掌由右向左在体前击右脚脚面。目视左掌(图5-54)。

(3) Keep moving, right foot falls, jump rightward and backward, turn 270°, right leg swings rightward, left leg falls, at the same time, right hand swings broad-

sword backward, broadsword blade upward, broadsword tip backward, left palm swings leftward to right instep. Look at left palm (Figure 5-54).

图 5-54(Figure 5-54)

（4）上动不停,左脚自然落地,身体右转180°,右脚向右后落步成弓步；同时,右手持刀经背部向前、向右下方拉刀置于右膝外侧,刀刃向下,刀尖斜向前；左掌随身体右转的力量向右摆置于右肩前,掌心向外,掌尖向上。目视左前方(图5-55)。

4) Keep moving, left foot falls, turn rightward 180°, right foot falls rightward into the bow stance, at the same time, right hand swings broadsword forward, rightward and downward to right knee outward via the back, broadsword blade downward, broadsword tip slantly forward, left palm against right shoulder, palm center outward, palm tip upward. Look leftward (Figure 5-55).

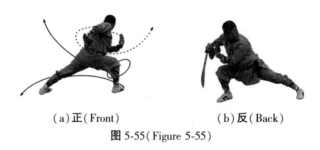

(a)正(Front)　　　　(b)反(Back)

图 5-55(Figure 5-55)

第三段

Section 3

29.箭弹刺刀

（1）身体左转,右腿向前一步成弓步；同时,右手持刀,手腕外旋向上撩刀,刀刃向上,刀尖向前。左掌向上摆击于体侧。目视刀尖(图 5-56)。

29. Spring broadsword stabbing

(1) Turn left, right leg strides one step into the bow stance, at the same time, right hand holds broadsword, turn wrist outward and thrust broadsword upward, broadsword blade upward, broadsword tip forward. Left palm swings to the sides. Look at broadsword tip (Figure 5-56).

图 5-56(Figure 5-56)

(2)上动不停,左脚向前一步,屈膝前弓;同时,右手腕外旋向上、向左、向下、向上撩刀,刀刃向上;左掌附于刀背上,向前推刀。目视前方(图 5-57)。

(2) Keep moving, left foot strides one step, bend knee into the front bow stance, at the same time, turn right wrist outward, thrust broadsword upward, leftward and downward, broadsword blade upward, left palm against broadsword back, push broadsword forward. Look straight ahead (Figure 5-57).

图 5-57(Figure 5-57)

(3)上动不停,右脚向前一步,脚尖外展;同时,右手持刀向前、向上、向后、向下劈刀,刀刃向下,刀尖向后;左掌向前摆击于体侧,掌心向前,掌指向上。目视刀尖(图5-58)。

(3) Keep moving, right foot strides one step, tiptoes outreach, bend knee into the front bow stance, at the same time, right hand chops broadsword forward, upward, backward and downward, broadsword blade downward, broadsword tip backward, left palm swings forward to the sides, palm center forward, fingers upward. Look at broadsword tip (Figure 5-58).

图5-58(Figure 5-58)

(4)上动不停,身体重心移至右腿,右脚蹬地向上弹踢,脚面绷直,左脚自然下垂;同时,右手持刀内旋向前、向上回收置胸前后,再向身体正前上方刺刀,刀刃向上,刀尖向前。左掌附于右手腕向体前摆臂。目视刀尖(图5-59)。

(4) Keep moving, shift gravity center to right leg, right foot falls and kicks upward, keep instep straight, left foot drops, at the same time, right hand swings broadsword forward and upward, close it to the chest, thrust it forward and upward, broadsword blade upward, broadsword tip forward. Look at broadsword tip (Figure 5-59).

图5-59(Figure 5-59)

30.弓步背刀

左脚自然落地,右脚向后落步,身体右转成弓步;同时,右手持刀,手腕内旋随转体向下劈刀后经体前向右、向上撩刀置于右肩上,刀背贴在右肩上,刀刃向上,刀尖向左前下方;左掌变勾手向下经腹前向上摆击于身体左侧。目视左前方(图5-60)。

30. Bow stance broadsword backing

Left foot falls, right foot retreats, turn right into the bow stance, at the same time, right hand holds broadsword, turn wrist inward, thrust broadsword rightward and upward, broadsword blade upward, broadsword tip leftward, forward and downward, change left palm into hook against the left side. Look leftward (Figure 5-60).

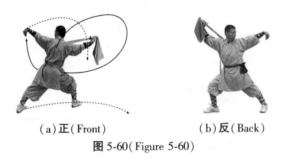

(a)正(Front)　　(b)反(Back)

图 5-60(Figure 5-60)

31.三劈刀

(1)左脚经右腿后向右插步,两腿弯曲下蹲成歇步;同时,右手持刀,向下、向右、经体前向左劈刀。左掌向右下方摆击于右臂前,掌心向右。目视刀身(图5-61)。

31. Three broadsword chopping

(1) Left foot strides rightward via right leg, squat into the sitting stance, at the same time, right hand swings broadsword downward, rightward, downward, leftward and upward, left palm swings downward to right arm. Look at broadsword (Figure 5-61).

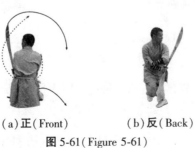

(a)正(Front)　　(b)反(Back)

图 5-61(Figure 5-61)

(2)上动不停,右脚向右一步,两腿屈膝下蹲成马步;同时,右手持刀向右下方劈刀;左掌由下向上架于头顶,掌心向上。目视刀尖(图5-62)。

(2) Keep moving, right foot strides rightward, bend knees and squat into the horse-riding stance, at the same time, right hand chops broadsword upward, rightward and downward, left palm supports overhead, supinely. Look at broadsword tip (Figure 5-62).

图5-62(Figure 5-62)

(3)上动不停,左脚经右腿后向右插步,两腿弯曲下蹲成歇步;同时,右手持刀,向下、向左劈刀,左掌向下摆击置于右臂前。目视刀尖(图5-63)。

(3) Keep moving, left foot strides rightward via right leg, squat into the sitting stance, at the same time, right hand swings broadsword downward, leftward and upward, left palm swings downward to right arm. Look at broadsword (Figure 5-63).

(a)正(Front)　　　(b)反(Back)

图5-63(Figure 5-63)

(4)上动不停,右脚向右一步,两腿屈膝下蹲成马步;同时,右手持刀向右下方劈刀;左掌由下向上架于头顶,掌心向上。目视刀尖(图5-64)。

(4) Keep moving, right foot strides one step rightward, bend knees and

squat into the horse-riding stance, at the same time, right hand chops broadsword upward, rightward and downward, left palm supports overhead, supinely. Look at broadsword tip (Figure 5-64).

图 5-64(Figure 5-64)

(5)上动不停,左脚经右腿后向右插步,两腿弯曲下蹲成歇步;同时,右手持刀向下、向左劈刀。左掌向下摆击置于右臂前。目视刀尖(图 5-65)。

(5) Keep moving, left foot strides rightward via right leg, squat into the sitting stance, at the same time, right hand swings broadsword downward, leftward and upward, left palm swings downward to right arm. Look at broadsword (Figure 5-65).

(a)正(Front)　　(b)反(Back)
图 5-65(Figure 5-65)

(6)上动不停,右脚向右一步,两腿屈膝下蹲成马步;同时,右手持刀向右下方劈刀;左掌由下向上架于头顶,掌心向上。目视刀尖(图 5-66)。

(6) Keep moving, right foot strides rightward, bend knees and squat into the horse-riding stance, at the same time, right hand chops broadsword upward, rightward and downward, left palm supports overhead, supinely. Look at broadsword tip (Figure 5-66).

图 5-66(Figure 5-66)

32.马步背刀

(1)身体上起左转 90°;同时,右手持刀,手腕内旋向下经后背向上、向下、再向上绕刀花一周置于体侧。左掌向下置于右臂肘关节内侧。目视刀刃(图 5-67)。

32. Horse-riding stance broadsword backing

(1) Arise and turn leftward 90°, at the same time, right hand holds broadsword, turn wrist inward, swing broadsword upward, downward and upward via the back, left palm downward against right elbow joint inward. Look at broadsword blade (Figure 5-67).

图 5-67(Figure 5-67)

(2)上动不停,身体右转 90°;同时,右手持刀,向下、向左、向上绕刀花,刀尖向上,刀刃向前。左掌附于右臂内侧肘关节处。目视刀尖(图 5-68)。

(2) Keep moving, turn rightward 90°, at the same time, right hand holds broadsword, swing it downward, leftward and upward, broadsword tip upward, broadsword blade forward, left palm against right elbow joints. Look at broadsword tip (Figure 5-68).

第五章 少林单刀

图 5-68（Figure 5-68）

（3）上动不停，身体向左转 90°，两腿屈膝下蹲成马步；同时，右手持刀，向左、向上绕刀一周后手腕外旋，刀身贴在身体背部，刀尖向上，刀刃向左前方。左掌附在右肩前。目视左掌（图 5-69）。

（3）Keep moving, turn leftward 90°, bend knees and squat into the horse-riding stance, at the same time, right hand holds broadsword, swing it leftward and upward a circle, swing wrist outward, broadsword against the back, broadsword tip upward, broadsword blade leftward and forward, left palm against right shoulder. Look at left palm (Figure 5-69).

（a）正（Front）　　　（b）反（Back）

图 5-69（Figure 5-69）

33.旋风脚马步背刀

（1）上动不停，右腿屈膝用力蹬地，身体腾空左转 180°右腿由外向里摆踢成旋风脚；同时，右手持刀，刀身贴于背部，刀尖向上。左掌在体前迎击右脚掌心。（图 5-70）。

33. Whirlwind kicking horse-riding stance broadsword backing

（1）Bend right knee and kick vigorously, jump and turn leftward 180° into whirlwind kicking, at the same time, right hand holds broadsword, broadsword against the back, broadsword tip upward (Figure 5-70).

图 5-70（Figure 5-70）

（2）上动不停,身体继续左转180°,两腿自然下落成马步;同时,右手持刀贴在身体后背,刀刃向左,刀尖向上。左掌拍击右脚掌后向下、向上架于头顶上方。目视右前方(图 5-71)。

（2）Keep moving, turn leftward 180°, legs fall into the horse-riding stance, at the same time, right hand holds broadsword against the back, broadsword blade leftward, broadsword tip upward, and left palm supports overhead. Look rightward and forward (Figure 5-71).

图 5-71（Figure 5-71）

34.绞刀提膝

（1）身体右转90°,右手持刀向下、向上在背后绕刀一周置体侧,刀刃向前,刀尖向上,同时左掌附于右手腕处。目随刀走(图 5-72)。

34. Broadsword twisting and knee lifting

（1）Turn rightward 90°, right hand holds broadsword, swing it downward and upward a circle, broadsword blade forward, broadsword tip upward. Look at broadsword (Figure 5-72).

第五章　少林单刀

图 5-72（Figure 5-72）

（2）上动不停，身体左转90°，右手持刀向下、向上绕刀一周，手腕外旋，刀身贴于身体背部，刀刃向左、刀尖向上，左手附于右臂前(图5-73)。

(2) Keep moving, turn leftward 90°, right hand holds broadsword, downward and upward a circle, swing wrist outward, broadsword against the back, broadsword blade leftward, broadsword tip upward, left hand against right arm (Figure 5-73).

图 5-73（Figure 5-73）

（3）上动不停，身体重心移至左腿，右腿屈膝提起，脚面绷直；同时，右手持刀向上翻腕360°置于身体右侧，刀刃向上，刀尖向下。左掌附在右手腕处。目视刀尖(图5-74)。

(3) Keep moving, shift gravity center to left leg, bend and lift right knee, keep instep straight, at the same time, right hand holds broadsword and turn wrist 360° rightward, broadsword blade upward, broadsword tip downward, left palm against right wrist. Look at broadsword tip (Figure 5-74).

205

(a)正(Front)　　　　(b)反(Back)

图 5-74(Figure 5-74)

35.回头望月刀

（1）右脚向前下方落步成右弓步；同时，右手持刀向右前下方刺刀，刀刃向下，刀尖向前。左掌向后摆掌。目视前下方(图 5-75)。

35. Back leg kicking broadsword

（1） Right foot falls into the bow stance, at the same time, right hand holds broadsword, stab it rightward, forward and downward, broadsword blade downward, broadsword tip forward, left palm push backward. Look forward and downward (Figure 5-75).

图 5-75(Figure 5-75)

（2）上动不停，左脚向前一步，身体右转 180°；同时，右手持刀向后扫刀，刀刃向右后前方，刀尖向右前方；左掌在体侧不动，掌心向左后前方。目视刀尖(图 5-76)。

（2） Keep moving, left foot strides one step, turn rightward 180°, at the same time, right hand sweeps broadsword backward, broadsword blade rightward, backward and forward, broadsword tip rightward and forward, keep left palm still against the side, palm center leftward, backward and forward. Look at broadsword tip (Figure 5-76).

图 5-76(Figure 5-76)

(3)上动不停,身体重心移至左腿,右腿提膝身体右转180°;同时,右手持刀,手腕外旋向后平扫,绕后脑一周贴于左肩上。左掌随身体摆动置于体侧。目视左前方(图5-77)。

(3) Keep moving, shift gravity center to left leg, lift right knee, turn rightward 180°, at the same time, right hand holds broadsword, twist wrist outward and swing broadsword backward a circle against left shoulder, swing left palm against the side. Look leftward (Figure 5-77).

图 5-77(Figure 5-77)

(4)上动不停,右脚向前落步前弓成右弓步;同时,右手持刀从左肩外侧向胸前拉刀,刀刃向上,刀尖斜向下,刀背贴于左臂;左臂弯曲,左掌护在右手腕上。目视左前方(图5-78)。

(4) Keep moving, right foot falls into the bow stance, at the same time, right hand pulls broadsword to the chest from left shoulder outward, broadsword blade upward, broadsword tip downward, broadsword backing against left arm, bend left arm, make left palm protect the right wrist.

Look leftward (Figure 5-78).

图 5-78(Figure 5-78)

第四段

Section 4

36.马步磨盘刀

(1)右脚向前一步,身体左转180°下蹲成半马步;同时,右手持刀向上、向后绕背部向左前方下扫刀。左臂随刀缠头时向身体左侧摆掌,掌心向上。目视刀尖(图 5-79)。

36. Horse-riding stance millstone broadsword

(1) Right foot strides one step, turn leftward 180° into a bow and horse-riding stance, at the same time, right hand sweeps broadsword upward, backward, and leftward and forward, at the same time, left arm pushes leftward. Look at broadsword tip (Figure 5-79).

图 5-79(Figure 5-79)

(2)上动不停,身体继续左转180°,左脚向右后退步;同时,右手持刀继续向左贴地面平扫,左掌摆至体侧不动。目视刀尖(图5-80)。

(2) Keep moving, turn leftward 180°, left foot retreats rightward and backward, at the same time, right left hand sweeps broadsword against the floor. Look at broadsword tip (Figure 5-80).

图 5-80(Figure 5-80)

(3)上动不停,身体左转90°,两脚向左碾地成左弓步;同时,右手持刀向前、向左、向后扫刀;左掌上架于头顶,刀刃向左,刀尖向后,掌心向上。目视前方(图5-81)。

(3) Keep moving, turn leftward 90°, feet grind leftward into the left bow stance, at the same time, right hand sweeps broadsword forward, leftward and backward, parry left palm overhead, broadsword blade leftward, broadsword tip backward, supinely. Look straight ahead (Figure 5-81).

图 5-81(Figure 5-81)

37.单拍脚虚步藏刀

(1)右脚向前上方弹踢,脚面绷直;同时,右手持刀不变,左掌从头顶上方向下拍击右脚面。目视前方(图5-82)。

37. Single batting empty stance broadsword hiding

(1) Right foot kicks forward, keep instep straight, at the same time, right hand holds broadsword, left palm pats right instep from overhead. Look straight ahead (Figure 5-82).

图 5-82(Figure 5-82)

(2)上动不停,右脚向后下落地,身体右转180°成右弓步;同时,右手持刀随身体右转向后平扫,左掌向后推击。目视刀尖(图5-83)。

(2) Keep moving, right foot falls backward, turn rightward 180° into the right bow stance, at the same time, right hand sweeps broadsword backward, left palm pushes backward. Look at broadsword tip (Figure 5-83).

图 5-83(Figure 5-83)

(3)左脚向前一步,身体右转180°,右脚向后退半步;同时,右手持刀,向后平扫,刀刃向右,刀尖向前。左掌随身体转动摆击于体侧。目视前方(图5-84)。

(3) Left foot strides one step, turn rightward 180°, right foot retreats half a step, at the same time, right hand sweeps broadsword backward, broadsword blade rightward, broadsword tip forward, left palm swings inward. Look straight

ahead (Figure 5-84).

图 5-84(Figure 5-84)

（4）上动不停，身体重心移至右腿，左脚后退半步；同时，右手持刀上举使刀经背部绕于左肩后，刀尖向下，刀刃向后；左掌向里屈臂收于胸前，掌心向右，掌指向上。目视前方(图 5-85)。

(4) Keep moving, shift gravity center to right leg, left foot retreats half a step, at the same time, right hand lifts broadsword, make it behind left shoulder, broadsword tip downward, broadsword blade backward, close left arm inward and in front of the chest, palm rightward, fingers upward. Look straight ahead (Figure 5-85).

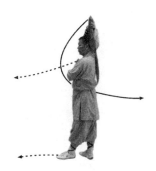

图 5-85(Figure 5-85)

（5）上动不停，右腿屈膝半蹲，左脚向前半步，脚尖点地成左虚步；同时，右手持刀绕后脑向右下方带刀，刀刃斜向后，刀尖斜向下。左掌向前推出。目视左掌(图 5-86)。

(5) Keep moving, bend right knee on semi-crouch balance, left foot strides half a step, tiptoes touchdown into the left empty stance, at the same

time, right hand swings broadsword rightward from the back, broadsword blade obliquely backward, broadsword tip slantingly downward. Left palm pushes forward. Look at left palm (Figure 5-86).

图 5-86(Figure 5-86)

38.蹲步抱刀

(1)右脚向前一步成右弓步;同时,右手持刀向前斜上方刺刀。左掌向前附在右手腕上。目视刀尖(图 5-87)。

38. Squatting and broadsword tackling

(1) Right foot strides one step into the bow stance, at the same time, right hand stabs broadsword forward and obliquely upward, left palm forward and against right wrist. Look at broadsword tip (Figure 5-87).

图 5-87(Figure 5-87)

(2)上动不停,身体左转180°,左脚在前,右手持刀上举,经头顶绕刀向下收于左肩侧。左掌附于右小臂内侧。目视前方(图 5-88)。

(2) Keep moving, turn leftward 180°, left foot in the front, right hand lifts broadsword, close it to left shoulder via overhead, left palm against right

forearm inward. Look straight ahead (Figure 5-88).

图 5-88(Figure 5-88)

(3)上动不停,右脚向左脚内侧上一步成并步,两腿屈膝下蹲;同时,右手持刀向腹前收刀,左手接刀,右掌附在刀柄。目视前下方(图 5-89)。

(3) Keep moving, right foot strides to the left foot inward into step touch, bend knees and squat, at the same time, right hand closes broadsword to the abdomen, left hand picks broadsword, right palm against broadsword handle. Look forward and downward (Figure 5-89).

图 5-89(Figure 5-89)

39.二起飞脚

右脚蹬地,身体腾空,左腿自然伸直,右脚向上弹击,脚面绷直;右掌从腰间向上,迎击右脚面,左手抱刀不变。目视前方(图 5-90)。

39. Double flying and kicking

Feet fall simultaneously, jump, left leg straight, right foot kicks upward, keep instep straight, right palm resists right instep from the waist, left hand holds broadsword. Look straight ahead (Figure 5-90).

图 5-90(Figure 5-90)

40.马步架拳抱刀

(1)上动不停,身体右转;同时,右腿自然下落向下震脚,左腿在右脚下落震地时随即上提,左手抱刀向上摆击置于身体左侧,右掌变拳向右下方摆击于体侧。目视右拳(图 5-91)。

40. Horse-riding stance broadsword tackling

(1) Keep moving, turn rightward, at the same time, lift right foot and make it stamp, bend and lift left knee, left hand swings broadsword upward and leftward, right fist swings rightward, fist center upward. Look at right fist (Figure 5-91).

图 5-91(Figure 5-91)

(2)上动不停,左脚向左前方落步,两腿屈膝下蹲成马步;左手抱刀向下收抱于腹前,刀刃向上,刀尖向前;右拳屈臂上架于头上方,拳心向上。目视左前方发出"威"的声音(图 5-92)。

(2) Keep moving, left foot strides one step leftward and falls, bend knees and squat into the horse-riding stance, left hand holds broadsword downward and against the abdomen, broadsword blade upward, broadsword tip forward, bend right arm and make it overhead, fist center upward. Look leftward (Figure 5-92).

图 5-92(Figure 5-92)

41.并步抱刀

接上势,身体上起,左脚向右收一步,左手抱刀收于腰间,右拳向下收抱腰间。目视正前方(图 5-93)。

41. Step touch broadsword tackling

Keep moving, arise, left foot strides one step rightward, left hand holds broadsword against the waist, close right fist downward and against the waist. Look straight ahead (Figure 5-93).

图 5-93(Figure 5-93)

42.收势

接上势,左手抱刀自然下垂于体侧,右掌下垂于右侧,掌心向内贴于大腿外侧。目视前方(图5-94)。

42. Closing

Keep moving, left-hand holds -broadsword and falls, right palm hangs rightward, palm center against leg outward. Look straight ahead (Figure 5-94).

图 5-94(Figure 5-94)

第六章　少林十三枪
Chapter 6　Shaolin 13-Spear

第一节　套路动作名称
Quarter 1　Routine Name

第一段
Section 1

1. 预备势(Preparation)
2. 开步抱拳(Holding fists with feet apart)
3. 丁步拖枪(T-step spear dragging)
4. 弓步拦拿扎枪(Bow stance spear stopping, taking and stabbing)
5. 虚步绞拨枪(Empty stance spear twisting and poking)
6. 跳步拦拿扎枪(Jumping and spear stopping, taking and stabbing)
7. 舞花扎枪(Spear waving and stabbing)
8. 虚步架枪(Empty stance spear parrying)

第二段
Section 2

9. 跳步弓步扎枪(Jumping bow stance spear stabbing)
10. 舞花跳马步劈枪(Waving and jumping horse-riding stance spear chopping)
11. 翻身弓步扎枪(Rolling bow stance spear stabbing)
12. 转身下扎枪(Turning and downward spear stabbing)
13. 虚步挑把枪(Empty stance spear tilting)

14. 弓步右挑枪(Bow stance rightward spear tilting)
15. 弓步左压枪(Bow stance leftward spear pressing)
16. 弓步拦拿扎枪(Bow stance spear stopping, taking and stabbing)

第三段

Section 3

17. 翻身盖把下戳枪(Rolling and capping downward spear poking)
18. 舞花平托枪(Spear waving and holding)
19. 翻身拦拿扎枪(Rolling and spear stopping, taking and stabbing)
20. 提膝下拨枪(Knee lifting downward spear stirring)
21. 翻身弓步扎枪(Turning bow stance spear stabbing)

第四段

Section 4

22. 绕喉拿扎枪(Spear winding and stabbing)
23. 舞花翻身马步劈枪(Waving and rolling horse-riding spear chopping)
24. 反身跳弓步扎枪(Turning and jumping bow stance spear stabbing)
25. 翻腰拦拿扎枪(Waist turning spear stopping, taking and stabbing)
26. 二起脚架拳背枪(Double kicking fist holding and spear backing)
27. 并步抱拳(Stance touch fist holding)
28. 收势(Closing)

第二节　动作说明

Quarter 2　Movement Descriptions

第一段

Section 1

1.预备势

两脚并立,右手握枪置于体侧,枪把着地;左手五指并拢垂于身体左侧。目视前方(图6-1)。

1. Preparation

Feet parallel, right hand holds spear against the side, spear handle touchdown, left palm flat against the left side. Look straight ahead (Figure 6-1).

图 6-1(Figure 6-1)

2. 开步抱拳

接上势,左掌变拳,向上抱于腰间;同时,左脚向左跨半步,向左摆头。目视左前方(图6-2)。

2. Holding fists with feet apart

Keep moving, change left palm into fist, upward against the waist, at the same time, left foot strides half a step leftward, turn left. Look leftward (Figure 6-2).

图 6-2(Figure 6-2)

3.丁步拖枪

右脚外侧向右踢后自然屈膝下落,左脚向右脚内侧收步成丁字步;同时,右手向下滑枪握住把端收于腰间,左手持枪内旋成拿枪。目视枪尖

219

(图 6-3)。

3.T-step spear dragging

Right foot kicks outward, bend elbow and fall, close left foot to right foot inward into the T-step, at the same time, right hand holds spear handle end against the waist, left hand takes spear. Look at the spear tip (Figure 6-3).

图 6-3(Figure 6-3)

4.弓步拦拿扎枪

(1)左脚上前一步,两腿屈膝下蹲成马步;同时,右手握把上翻,左手持枪外翻拦枪(图 6-4)。

4. Bow stance spear stopping, taking and stabbing

(1) Left foot strides forward, bend knees and squat into the horse-riding stance, at the same time, right hand turns upward, left hand turns spear to stop (Figure 6-4).

图 6-4(Figure 6-4)

(2)上动不停,右手握把下压收于腰间,左手持枪内扣拿枪(图 6-5)。

(2) Keep moving, right hand presses spear handle against the waist, left hand buckles inward to take spear (Figure 6-5).

图 6-5（Figure 6-5）

（3）上动不停,两脚向左碾地,身体左转成左弓步;同时,右手推把向前扎枪。目视枪尖(图 6-6)。

(3) Keep moving, feet grind leftward, turn left into the left bow stance, at the same time, and right hand pushes forward to stab spear. Look at the spear tip (Figure 6-6).

图 6-6（Figure 6-6）

5. 虚步绞拨枪

身体重心移至右腿,左脚向后收半步,脚尖点地,成左虚步;同时,右手持枪回拉向上抽抱架于头顶,左手向前滑把;枪身从上由内向外拨枪。目视前方(图 6-7)。

5. Empty stance spear twisting and poking

Shift gravity center to right leg, close left foot half a step, tiptoes touchdown into the left empty stance, at the same time, right hand swings spear backward and upward, left hand slides forward, swing spear outward. Look straight ahead (Figure 6-7).

图 6-7（Figure 6-7）

6. 跳步拦拿扎枪

（1）左脚向前半步成马步；同时，右手握把向下收于腰间（图 6-8）。

6. Jumping and spear stopping, taking and stabbing

(1) Left foot strides half a step forward into the horse-riding stance, at the same time, close right hand against the waist (Figure 6-8).

图 6-8（Figure 6-8）

（2）上动不停，右脚蹬地向前跳步，左脚面内扣于右腿膝关节后；同时，右手握把内旋屈肘向上翻至右肩前方，左手持枪外翻拦枪（图 6-9）。

(2) Keep moving, right foot stamps and jumps, left instep buckles inward to right knee, at the same time, right hand turns inward, bend elbow upward to right shoulder, left hand turns outward to stop (Figure 6-9).

图 6-9（Figure 6-9）

(3)上动不停,左脚向前落成马步,右手握把下翻收于腰间,左手持枪内扣拿枪(图 6-10)。

(3) Keep moving, left foot falls forward into the horse-riding stance, close right hand against the waist, left hand buckles inward to take spear (Figure 6-10).

图 6-10(Figure 6-10)

(4)上动不停,身体左转 90°成左弓步;同时,右手推把向前扎枪。目视枪尖(图 6-11)。

(4) Keep moving, turn leftward 90° into the left bow stance, at the same time, right hand pushes to stab spear. Look at the spear tip (Figure 6-11).

图 6-11(Figure 6-11)

7. 舞花扎枪

(1)右腿向前半步,身体左转;同时,两手滑枪,枪尖向下、向后、向上舞花(图 6-12)。

7.Spear waving and stabbing

(1) Right leg strides forwards half a step, turn left, at the same time, hands slip spear, wave spear tip downward, backward and upward (Figure 6-12).

图 6-12（Figure 6-12）

（2）上动不停,身体左转 90°,右腿前提,右脚扣在左腿膝关节后侧;同时,两手持枪留把继续向前舞花,使枪至身体前方,枪尖向前。目视前方(图 6-13)。

（2）Keep moving, turn leftward 90°, lift right leg forward, right foot buckles to left knee inward, at the same time, hands hold spear and wave it, spear forward, spear tip forward. Look straight ahead (Figure 6-13).

图 6-13（Figure 6-13）

（3）上动不停,右脚向前下落成右弓步;同时,右手推把向前扎枪,高与肩平。目视枪尖(图 6-14)。

（3）Keep moving, right foot falls forward into the bow stance, at the same time, right hand pushes forward to stab spear, keep at the shoulder's level. Look at the spear tip (Figure 6-14).

图 6-14（Figure 6-14）

第六章　少林十三枪

8. 虚步架枪

身体左转270°,左腿屈膝下蹲,右脚尖点地成右虚步;同时,右手向前滑枪从身体左后方绕行一周后由上向下点枪,左手持把架于头顶上方。目视前方(图6-15)。

8.Empty stance spear parrying

Turn leftward 270°, bend left knee and squat, right tiptoes touchdown into the right empty stance, at the same time, right hand slips spear forward, swing it a circle, point it downward, left hand overhead. Look straight ahead (Figure 6-15).

图 6-15(Figure 6-15)

第二段

Section 2

9. 跳步弓步扎枪

(1)左脚向前垫步,右脚向前提膝;同时,两手持枪回收拉于体前,目视枪尖(图6-16)。

9. Jumping bow stance spear stabbing

(1) Left foot take a skip step forward bend , and lift right knee, at the same time, hands pull spear backward, look at spear tip (Figure 6-16).

图 6-16（Figure 6-16）

（2）上动不停,右脚向前下方落步成弓步;同时,两手持枪滑把向前扎枪。目视前方(图 6-17)。

(2) Keep on moving, right foot falls forward into the horse-riding stance, at the same time, hands slip and stab spear forward. Look straight ahead (Figure 6-17).

图 6-17（Figure 6-17）

10. 舞花跳马步劈枪

（1）身体向后左转 180°;同时,两手握把滑至枪身中段,使枪尖随转体向上、向下划弧。目视枪尖(图 6-18)。

10. Waving and jumping horse-riding stance spear chopping

(1) Turn backward and leftward 180°, at the same time, hands slip to spear center, make spear tip draw curve upward and downward. Look at the spear tip (Figure 6-18).

图 6-18（Figure 6-18）

（2）上动不停,右脚向前一步,两腿屈膝下蹲成马步；同时,两手抱枪使枪尖向后、向上、向下划弧于体前,枪尖向右前方(图6-19)。

(2) Keep moving, right foot strides one step forward, bend knees and squat into the horse-riding stance, at the same time, hands hold spear, make spear tip draw curve backward, upward and downward, spear tip rightward and forward (Figure 6-19).

图 6-19（Figure 6-19）

（3）上动不停,右脚蹬地跳起,身体腾空左转180°；同时,两手持枪随转体由下向右、向上举于头上方(图6-20)。

(3) Keep moving, right foot jumps, turn leftward 180°, at the same time, hands hold spear and swing it rightward, upward and overhead (Figure 6-20).

图 6-20（Figure 6-20）

（4）上动不停，身体继续左转180°，两脚先左后右，依次落地成马步；同时，左手握抱下压收于腰间；右手持枪随落步向右、向下劈枪。目视枪尖（图6-21）。

（4）Keep moving, turn leftward 180°, feet fall leftward and rightward into the horse-riding stance, at the same time, close left hand against the waist, right hand chops spear rightward and downward. Look at the spear tip (Figure 6-21).

图6-21(Figure 6-21)

11. 翻身弓步扎枪

（1）左腿向右前上方提起，右腿蹬地腾空跳起。身体向右转180°，左腿自然下垂，右腿向上起膝成空中提膝势；同时，两手持枪随转体向上、向右后下扎枪。目视枪尖（图6-22）。

11. Rolling bow stance spear stabbing

（1）Lift left leg rightward, upward and forward, right leg stamps and jumps. Turn rightward 180°, left leg falls, lift right leg to the air, at the same time, hands hold spear and stab it upward, rightward and backward. Look at the spear tip (Figure 6-22).

图6-22(Figure 6-22)

第六章 少林十三枪

(2)上动不停,左脚落地,身体继续右转180°,右脚向前落地成右弓步;同时,右手推把向前扎枪,高与肩平。目视枪尖(图6-23)。

(2) Keep moving, left foot falls, turn rightward 180°, right foot falls into the right bow stance, at the same time, right hand pushes forward to stab spear, keep at the shoulder's level. Look at the spear tip (Figure 6-23).

图 6-23(Figure 6-23)

12. 转身下扎枪

(1)两脚向左碾地,身体左转成左弓步;同时,左手握把,右手滑把握于枪身中段,随身体左转力以腰带臂发力向左后上方点枪。目视枪尖(图6-24)。

12. Turning and downward spear stabbing

(1) Feet grind leftward, turn left into the left bow stance, at the same time, left hand holds spear, right hand holds spear center, swing it leftward, backward and upward. Look at the spear tip (Figure 6-24).

图 6-24(Figure 6-24)

(2)上动不停,身体右转270°,身体重心移至右腿,左脚点地成转身交叉步；同时，两手持枪向上、向下、划弧收于身体右侧，向右下方斜刺枪。目视枪尖（图 6-25）。

(2) Keep moving, turn rightward 270°, shift gravity center to right leg, left foot touchdown, turn into the cross stance, at the same time, hands hold spear and make it draw curve upward and downward, and obliquely rightward. Look at the spear tip (Figure 6-25).

图 6-25（Figure 6-25）

13. 虚步挑把枪

左脚向右前方上一步，身体右转，右脚随即经左腿向后撤一步，重心移至右腿，左脚尖点地；两腿屈膝下蹲成左虚步；同时，左手滑把向上留把，右手握于枪身中段向体前上架枪，枪尖向上。目视前方（图 6-26）。

13. Empty stance spear tilting

Left foot strides a step rightward and forward, turn rightward 360°, close right foot to left leg, shift gravity center to right leg, left tiptoes touchdown into the left empty stance, at the same time, left hand slips upward, right hand holds spear center and swing it forward, spear tip upward. Look straight ahead (Figure 6-26).

图 6-26（Figure 6-26）

14. 弓步右挑枪

(1)接上势,左脚向左前方上一步,身体上起,成站立势;同时,两手持枪向把端滑枪,枪尖向下划弧。目视枪尖(图 6-27)。

14. Bow stance rightward spear tilting

(1) Keep moving, left foot strides one step leftward and forward, stand, at the same time, hands hold spear, make it draw curve spear tip downward. Look at the spear tip (Figure 6-27).

图 6-27(Figure 6-27)

(2)上动不停,右腿向前上一步成右弓步;同时,两手向前滑把握于枪身中段使枪尖随身体转动,向上挑枪。目视左后方(图 6-28)。

(2) Keep moving, right leg strides one step leftward and forward into the right bow stance, at the same time, hands hold spear center and tilt it upward. Look leftward and backward (Figure 6-28).

图 6-28(Figure 6-28)

15. 弓步左压枪

身体右转 180°,左腿向右前方上一步成右弓步;同时,两手持枪身中段向下压枪,枪尖向右下方划弧。目视枪尖(图 6-29)。

15. Bow stance leftward spear pressing

Turn rightward 180°, left leg strides one step rightward and forward into the right bow stance, at the same time, hands hold spear center and press it, make it draw curve rightward and downward. Look at the spear tip (Figure 6-29).

图 6-29(Figure 6-29)

16. 弓步拦拿扎枪

（1）两脚碾地，身体右转180°，右脚在前，左脚在后，脚尖点地；同时，左手滑向把端，右手持枪中段，向后下方扎枪。目视枪尖(图6-30)。

16. Bow stance spear stopping, taking and stabbing

(1) Feet grind, turn rightward 180°, right foot in front, left foot behind, tiptoes touchdown, at the same time, left hand slips to the side, right hand holds spear center, make it stab backward and downward. Look at the spear tip (Figure 6-30).

图 6-30(Figure 6-30)

（2）上动不停，左脚向前收至右脚内侧；同时，右手向上、向前、向下滑至枪端握把下压于腰间，左手滑至枪中段。目视枪尖(图6-31)。

第六章　少林十三枪

(2) Keep moving, close left foot forward to right foot inward, at the same time, right hand presses spear upward, forward and downward and against the waist, left hand slips to spear center. Look at the spear tip (Figure 6-31).

图 6-31(Figure 6-31)

(3)接上势,左脚向前一步,两腿屈膝下蹲成马步;同时,左手持枪外翻拦枪。目视枪尖(图 6-32)。

(3) Keep moving, left foot strides one step forward, bend knees and squat into the horse-riding stance, at the same time, left hand turn outward to stop. Look at the spear tip (Figure 6-32).

图 6-32(Figure 6-32)

(4)上动不停,右手握把下压收于腰间,右手持枪,内扣拿枪。目视枪尖(图 6-33)。

(4) Keep moving, right hand against the waist, right hand buckles inward to take spear. Look at the spear tip (Figure 6-33).

图 6-33(Figure 6-33)

(5)上动不停,身体左转 90°成左弓步;同时,右手推把向左前扎枪。目视枪尖(图 6-34)。

(5) Keep moving, turn leftward 90° into the left bow stance, at the same time, right hand pushes forward and leftward to stab spear. Look at the spear tip (Figure 6-34).

图 6-34(Figure 6-34)

第三段

Section 3

17. 翻身盖把下戳枪

(1)身体重心移至左腿,右腿向前提膝;同时,左手向回抽枪握枪颈,右手向前滑把握于枪身中段,使枪尖向下划弧。目视前下方(图 6-35)。

17. Rolling and capping downward spear poking

(1) Shift gravity center to left leg, lift right knee, at the same time, left hand withdraws spear and holds spear neck, right hand holds spear center, make spear tip draw curve downward. Look forward and downward (Figure 6-35).

图 6-35(Figure 6-35)

（2）上动不停，右脚向前落步，两腿屈膝下蹲成马步；同时，左手握枪在腰间下压，右手握枪身中段向下压枪。目视枪把（图6-36）。

（2）Keep moving, right foot falls forward, bend knee and squat into the horse-riding stance, at the same time, left hand presses spear against the waist, right hand holds spear center and presses it downward. Look at spear handle (Figure 6-36).

图6-36（Figure 6-36）

（3）接上势，右脚向右后碾地，身体右转180°，左腿提膝；同时，两手持枪，随身体旋转时向上举过头顶再向下使枪身落于左肩上，枪尖向左下方。目视枪尖（图6-37）。

（3）Keep moving, right foot grinds rightward and backward, turn rightward 180°, lift left knee, at the same time, hands hold spear, swing spear upward and downward to left shoulder, spear tip downward and leftward. Look at the spear tip (Figure 6-37).

图6-37（Figure 6-37）

（4）左脚向前下方落步成左弓步；同时，两手持枪由上向前、向下戳枪，枪尖向下。目视枪尖（图6-38）。

（4）Left foot falls forward and downward into the left bow stance, at the same time, hands hold spear and poke is forward and downward, spear tip downward. Look at the spear tip (Figure 6-38).

图 6-38（Figure 6-38）

18. 舞花平托枪

（1）身体上起,右转 180°,重心移至左腿;同时,右手滑至枪身中段,使枪尖从下向上随身体转动向下轮臂划弧,左手变掌收于胸前。目视枪尖（图 6-39）。

18. Spear waving and holding

(1) Arise, turn rightward 180°, shift gravity center to left leg, at the same time, right hand slips to spear center, make spear tip draw curve downward, change left hand into palm against the chest. Look at the spear tip (Figure 6-39).

图 6-39（Figure 6-39）

（2）上动不停,右手持枪中段,枪随身体转动继续轮臂向下、向后、向上到头顶后再向体前下方划弧,枪尖朝下。目视右前方（图 6-40）。

(2) Keep moving, right hand holds spear center, swing it downward, backward and upward, and make it draw curve forward and downward, spear tip

downward. Look rightward and forward (Figure 6-40).

图 6-40(Figure 6-40)

(3)上动不停,右手持枪中段向上、向前轮臂划弧。目视枪尖(图6-41)。

(3) Keep moving, right hand holds spear center and make it draw curve upward, forward. Look at the spear tip (Figure 6-41).

图 6-41(Figure 6-41)

(4)接上势,身体右转90°,右手持枪回抽向下收于腰间,左手向前滑把握于枪身中段。目视枪尖(图6-42)。

(4) Keep moving, turn rightward 90°, right hand closes spear against the waist, left hand holds spear center. Look at the spear tip (Figure 6-42).

图 6-42 (Figure 6-42)

19. 翻身拦拿扎枪

（1）上动不停，左脚向前上一步，右脚随即向左脚后插步，两手持枪向下压枪，枪尖向左前下方。目视枪尖（图 6-43）。

19. Rolling and spear stopping, taking and stabbing

（1）Keep moving, left foot strides one step forward, right foot closes to left foot, hands hold spear and press it downward, spear tip leftward, forward and downward. Look at the spear tip（Figure 6-43）.

图 6-43（Figure 6-43）

（2）两脚向右碾地，身体右翻转 180°；同时，两手持枪使枪尖贴腿随身旋转，向左上方挑枪。目视枪尖（图 6-44）。

（2）Feet grind rightward, turn right 180°, at the same time, hands hold spear, make it against the leg and carry leftward and upward. Look at the spear tip（Figure 6-44）.

图 6-44（Figure 6-44）

（3）上动不停，身体继续右转 180°，右腿在前，左腿在后成交叉步；同时，右手握把下压，左手持枪中段向下劈枪。目视枪尖（图 6-45）。

（3）Keep moving, turn rightward 180°, right leg in front and left leg behind into the cross stance, at the same time, right hand presses spear downward, left hand hold spear center and chops it downward. Look at the spear tip (Figure 6-45).

图 6-45(Figure 6-45)

(4)接上势,左脚向前一步;同时,左手外翻成拦枪,右手握把。目视左前方(图 6-46)。

(4) Keep moving, left foot strides one step forward, at the same time, left hand turns to stop, and right hand holds spear. Look leftward and forward (Figure 6-46).

图 6-46(Figure 6-46)

(5)上动不停,两腿屈膝下蹲成马步;同时,右手握把向下收于腰间,左手持枪内旋成拿枪(图 6-47)。

(5) Keep moving, bend knees and squat into the horse-riding stance, at the same time, right hand against the waist, left hand swings spear inward (Figure 6-47).

239

图 6-47（Figure 6-47）

（6）上动不停,身体左转 90°成左弓步;同时,右手推把向前扎枪,高与肩平。目视枪尖(图 6-48)。

(6) Keep moving, turn leftward 90° into the left bow stance, at the same time, right hand pushes to stab spear, keep at the shoulder's level. Look at the spear tip (Figure 6-48).

图 6-48（Figure 6-48）

20. 提膝下拨枪

（1）右腿向前上一步,身体左转 90°,两腿屈膝下蹲成弓步;同时,左手滑至枪颈持枪,向下、向上屈肘于左腰间;右手滑至枪身中段使把向上、向前盖把。目视枪把(图 6-49)。

20. Knee lifting downward spear stirring

(1) Right leg strides one step forward, turn leftward 90°, bend knees and squat into the bow stance, at the same time, left hand slip to spear-neck and holds it, bend elbow downward, upward and against the left waist, right hand slip to spear center and swing it upward and forward. Look at spear handle (Figure 6-49).

第六章 少林十三枪

图 6-49（Figure 6-49）

（2）上动不停,重心向前移至右腿,左腿提膝;同时,左手持枪,向上、向前滑把握至枪身中段,向身体左下方拨枪;右手持枪附在左臂下方。目视枪尖(图 6-50)。

（2）Keep moving, shift gravity center to right leg, lift left knee, at the same time, left hand holds spear, and slips upward and forward to hold spear center, swing spear leftward and downward, right hand swings spear to left arm and downward. Look at the spear tip (Figure 6-50).

图 6-50（Figure 6-50）

21. 翻身弓步扎枪

（1）左脚向前下落,两手持枪不动。目视枪尖(图 6-51)。

21. Turning bow stance spear stabbing

（1）Left foot falls forward and downward, hands hold spear, keep still. Look at the spear tip (Figure 6-51).

图 6-51（Figure 6-51）

（2）接上势,左脚用力蹬地腾空上起,身体左转180°。左腿向上提膝,右腿自然下垂;同时,两手持枪随身体转动枪尖向上、向后、向下划弧。目视左前方(图6-52)。

(2) Keep moving, left foot jumps, turn leftward 180°, lift left knee, right leg falls, at the same time, hands hold spear, make spear draw curve upward, backward and downward. Look leftward (Figure 6-52).

图 6-52（Figure 6-52）

（3）上动不停,右脚自然下落,身体向左转270°,左脚向前落步,两腿屈膝下蹲成马步;同时,两手持枪随身体左转向下、向前,内扣拿枪。目视枪尖(图6-53)。

(3) Keep moving, right foot falls, turn leftward 270°, left foot falls forward, bend knees and squat into the horse-riding stance, at the same time, hands hold spear and swing it downward, forward and inward. Look at the spear tip (Figure 6-53).

图 6-53（Figure 6-53）

（4）接上势,身体左转 90°成左弓步;同时,右手推把向前扎枪。目视枪尖(图 6-54)。

(4) Keep moving, turn leftward 90° into the left bow stance, at the same time, right hand pushes forward to stab spear. Look at the spear tip (Figure 6-54).

图 6-54（Figure 6-54）

第四段

Section 4

22. 绕喉拿扎枪

（1）身体上起右转 180°,重心移至左腿,右脚尖点地;同时,左手持枪向右滑枪,握于枪颈,右手托枪身,随转体向右推送,枪尖与肩平。目视枪身(图 6-55)。

22. Spear winding and stabbing

(1) Stand and turn rightward 180°, shift gravity center to left leg, right

tiptoes touchdown, at the same time, left hand holds spear and slips it to right hand, holds spear neck, and right hand supports spear, turn rightward to push spear tip, keep at the shoulder's level. Look at spear (Figure 6-55).

图 6-55(Figure 6-55)

（2）接上势,右手握枪颈,左手接托枪身,使枪尖经咽喉向后穿出,枪与肩平。目视前方(图 6-56)。

(2) Keep moving, and right hand holds spear neck, left hand takes spear, thrust spear tip backward via throat, keep spear at the shoulder's level. Look straight ahead (Figure 6-56).

图 6-56(Figure 6-56)

（3）上动不停,右脚向后一步,身体右转 90°,两腿屈膝下蹲成马步;同时,右手握枪颈向后前方扎枪,滑把至枪身中段,左手向前滑枪握住枪把向下收于腰间。目视枪尖(图 6-57)。

(3) Keep moving, right foot retreats one step, turn rightward 90°, bend knees and squat into the horse-riding stance, at the same time, right hand holds spear-neck and stabs it backward and forward, slips to spear center, left hand

closes spear handle against waist. Look at the spear tip (Figure 6-57).

图 6-57(Figure 6-57)

(4)两脚向右碾地,身体右转成右弓步;同时,左手推把向前扎枪,高与肩平。目视枪尖(图 6-58)。

(4) Turn rightward into the right bow stance, at the same time, left hand pushes and stabs spear, keep at the shoulder's level. Look at the spear tip (Figure 6-58).

图 6-58(Figure 6-58)

23. 舞花翻身马步劈枪

(1)身体上起以左脚掌为轴,向左后转 270°,右脚尖点地;同时,两手向后抽枪,右手在前,左手在后握枪中段,使枪尖向上、向前、向下划弧。目视枪尖(图 6-59)。

23. Waving and rolling horse-riding spear chopping

(1) Arise, turn leftward 270° with left sole as the axis, right tiptoes touchdown, at the same time, hands pull spear backward, right hand in front, left hand behind, holds spear center, make spear tip draw curve upward, for-

ward and downward. Look at the spear tip (Figure 6-59).

图 6-59（Figure 6-59）

（2）上动不停,身体继续左转,右脚向前一步,两腿屈膝下蹲成马步;同时,两手持枪使枪尖经左腿外侧向后、向上、向前、向下划弧。目视枪尖(图6-60)。

（2）Keep moving, turn left, right foot strides one step forward, bend knees and squat into the horse-riding stance, at the same time, hands hold spear, make spear tip draw curve backward, upward, forward and downward. Look at the spear tip (Figure 6-60).

图 6-60（Figure 6-60）

（3）上动不停,右脚蹬地跳起,身体腾空左转180°;同时,两手持枪随转体由下向左、向上举于头上方。目视前下方(图6-61)。

（3）Keep moving, right foot jumps, turn leftward 180°, at the same time, hands hold spear, swing it leftward, upward and overhead. Look forward and downward (Figure 6-61).

图 6-61（Figure 6-61）

（4）上动不停,身体继续左转 90°,两脚先左后右依次落地成马步;同时,左手握把下压收于腰间,右手持枪随落步向右、向下劈枪。目视枪尖（图 6-62）。

(4) Keep moving, turn leftward 90°, feet fall into the horse-riding stance, at the same time, left hand closes it against the waist, right hand chops spear rightward and downward. Look at the spear tip (Figure 6-62).

图 6-62（Figure 6-62）

24. 反身跳弓步扎枪

（1）身体右转 90°,左腿屈膝上提,右腿挺膝直立;同时,左手握把端,右手握枪中段使枪尖随体转向上、向右划弧。目视前方（图 6-63）。

24. Turning and jumping bow stance spear stabbing

(1) Turn rightward 90°, bend and lift left knee, lift right knee and stand, at the same time, left hand holds spear end, right hand holds spear center, make spear tip draw curve upward and rightward. Look straight ahead (Figure 6-63).

图 6-63（Figure 6-63）

（2）上动不停，右脚蹬地跳起，身体腾空右转；同时，两手持枪随体向下划弧。目视枪尖（图6-64）。

(2) Keep moving, right foot jumps, turn right, at the same time, hands hold spear, make it draw curve downward. Look at the spear tip (Figure 6-64).

图 6-64（Figure 6-64）

（3）接上势，身体继续右转，两脚先左后右依次落地成右弓步；同时，左手向前推把扎枪。目视枪尖（图6-65）。

(3) Keep moving, turn right, feet fall into the right bow stance, at the same time, left hand pushes forward to stab spear. Look at the spear tip (Figure 6- 65).

图 6-65（Figure 6- 65）

25.翻腰拦拿扎枪

（1）身体向后左转270°；同时，两手持枪向前滑把至枪身中段，使枪尖随转体向上、向下划弧。目视枪尖（图6-66）。

25.Waist turning spear stopping, taking and stabbing

(1) Turn backward and leftward 270°, at the same time, hands slip to spear center, make spear tip draw curve upward and downward. Look at the spear tip (Figure 6-66).

图 6-66（Figure 6-66）

（2）上动不停，右脚向前一步，两腿屈膝下蹲成马步；同时，两手持枪使枪尖向后、向上、向下划弧于体前，枪尖向右前方（图 6-67）。

(2) Keep moving, right foot strides one step forward, bend knees and squat into the horse-riding stance, at the same time, hands hold spear, make spear tip draw curve backward, upward and downward, spear tip rightward and forward (Figure 6-67).

图 6-67（Figure 6-67）

（3）上动不停，右脚蹬地跳起，身体腾空左转180°；同时，两手持枪随转体由下向右、向上划弧（图 6-68）。

(3) Keep moving, right foot jumps, turn leftward 180°, at the same time, hands hold spear and swing it rightward, upward and overhead (Figure 6-68).

图 6-68（Figure 6-68）

（4）上动不停，身体继续左转180°，两脚先左后右依次落地成马步；同时，左手握把下压收于腰间；右手持枪随落步向右、向下劈枪。目视枪尖（图6-69）。

(4) Keep moving, turn leftward 180°, feet fall leftward and rightward into the horse-riding stance, at the same time, close left hand against the waist, right hand chops spear rightward and downward. Look at the spear tip (Figure 6-69).

图6-69（Figure 6-69）

（5）左脚向前一步，身体右转180°；同时，两手持枪滑把向内拦枪。目视枪尖（图6-70）。上动不停，两腿屈膝下蹲成后马步；同时，向内拿枪。目视枪尖（图6-71）。

(5) Left leg strides one step, turn leftward 180°, at the same time, hands hold spear to stop inward. Look at the spear tip (Figure 6-70). Keep moving, bend knees and squat into the bow stance, at the same time, right hand buckles spear inward. Look at the spear tip (Figure 6-71).

图6-70（Figure 6-70）　　图6-71（Figure 6-71）

（6）接上势，身体左转90°成左弓步；同时，右手推把向前扎枪，高与肩平。目视枪尖（图6-72）。

(6) Keep moving, turn leftward 90° into the left bow stance, at the same time, right hand pushes forward to stab spear, keep at the shoulder's level. Look at the spear tip (Figure 6-72).

图 6-72（Figure 6-72）

26.二起脚架拳背枪

（1）身体右转 90°；同时，右手握把滑至枪身中段，枪尖随转体向上、向前划弧使枪身置于左腋下，枪尖向前。目视左下方（图 6-73）。

26.Double kicking fist holding and spear backing

（1）Turn rightward 90°, at the same time, right hand holds spear center, make spear tip draw curve upward and forward and against left armpit, spear tip forward. Look leftward and downward (Figure 6-73).

图 6-73（Figure 6-73）

（2）上动不停，右脚用力蹬地，身体腾空，左脚由屈到伸向上弹踢，脚面绷直；同时，右手脱把向前插掌迎击右脚面，高与肩平，左手持枪中段，使枪尖向下运行成背枪。目视右手（图 6-74）。

（2）Keep moving, right foot stamps, jump, left foot kicks upward, keep instep straight, at the same time, right hand resists right instep, keep at the shoulder's level, left hand holds spear center, spear tip downward. Look at right hand (Figure 6-74).

图 6-74（Figure 6-74）

（3）上动不停，两脚先左后右依次落步，右脚向前落成右弓步，身体左转约90°；同时，右掌变拳经腹前上架于右肩前，拳心向下，枪尖斜向左下方。目视左后前方(图 6-75)。

(3) Keep moving, feet fall, right foot falls forward into the bow stance, turn leftward about 90°, at the same time, change right palm into fist against the abdomen, parry it against right shoulder, palm center downward, spear tip obliquely leftward and downward. Look leftward, backward and forward (Figure 6-75).

图 6-75（Figure 6-75）

27. 并步抱拳

（1）接上势，右腿向后撤一步，屈膝微下蹲成左高虚步。右手从左腋下接握枪把，使枪尖向下、向右经左腿外侧向前挑枪。目视前方(图 6-76)。

27. Stance touch fist holding

(1) Keep moving, right leg moves backward one step and slightly bends

into the left empty stance. Right hand catches and holds spear below left armpit, to make the spear tip downward and rightward and tilt spear forward. Look straight ahead (Figure 6-76).

图 6-76(Figure 6-76)

(2)上动不停,身体右转 90°,左脚尖点地;同时,两手持枪使枪把向下落于右腿外侧。目视枪身(图 6-77)。

(2) Keep moving, turn rightward 90°, left tiptoes touchdown, at the same time, hands hold spear and swing it to right leg outward. Look at spear (Figure 6-77).

图 6-77(Figure 6-77)

(3)接上势不停,身体左转 90°,左脚向右一步并步直立;同时,左手变拳收于腰间,右手持枪中段使枪贴身体右侧直立。目视左前方(图 6-78)。

(3) Keep moving, turn leftward 90°, left foot strides one step rightward and make step touch upright, at the same time, change left hand into fist against the waist, right hand holds spear center rightward and upright. Look leftward (Figure 6-78).

253

图 6-78(Figure 6-78)

28. 收势

接上势,左拳变掌,自然下垂于体侧。目视前方(图 6-79)。

28. Closing

Keep moving, change left fist into palm against the side. Look straight ahead (Figure 6-79).

图 6-79(Figure 6-79)